Mountains, Mozart, Manacles, Moose & Martinis

by

Roy Jacques

(Alias Jax; H.M. of M.H.S, C.C.E.with G.P. & O.M.M.)

PublishAmerica
Baltimore

ISBN: 1-4137-6827-X
PUBLISHED BY PUBLISHAMERICA, LLLP
www.publishamerica.com
Baltimore

Printed in the United States of America

DEDICATION AND ACKNOWLEDGMENTS

I would like to acknowledge Arvid Pedersen (dubbed by me "Great Dane," for his assistance in designing the book cover and for his contribution to my "alias." Whilst I have long been known as "Jax," it is Arvid who has awarded me the degrees of "Honorary Member of Moose Hunters Society (H.M. of M.H.S.), Camp Cook Extraordinaire, with Garlic Privileges (C.C.E. with G.P.) and Official Martini Mixer (O.M.M.)." Mr. Pedersen is now one of my annual hunting fraternity.

Another member of the present day annual hunter trek crew to whom this book is dedicated is Trevor Slack, son of one of the earlier members of said fraternity, Roy Slack, who, together with Rod Heinecky and Alf "Ancient Mariner" Poole have in recent years departed for the happy hunting grounds.

I must also acknowledge Tigger's sister Andrea, "Miss Thimbles," who bravely with her Mum, "Her Royal Highness," ventured into Chilcotin once, as mentioned in Chapter Twelve, never to return!

The book itself must needs be dedicated to "Her Royal Highness," my wife Lila, who for more than four decades has allowed me to abandon her annually to trek away on hunting and fishing jaunts and, for many of those years, to take along our son, the Tigger.

Finally, that same Tigger, my son Dan Jacques, must be acknowledged for shooting the picture at the close of Chapter One, which captures so brilliantly a stormy fall sky above the Timothy Meadow cabin. Other pictures are from my own collection, taken by self and friends during these annual jaunts, or by cameramen who accompanied me on my news-gathering efforts in Germany and Israel.

FOREWORD

There is only one Roy Jacques, and I am delighted that he has seen fit to preserve his unique style in this memoir. Buckle your seatbelts and hang on to your hats as you enjoy the ride of his life. One of Canada's top commentators in the second half of the twentieth century, "Jax" will reveal why politicians, labour leaders, businessmen, the high and mighty, and folks like you and me eagerly tuned into his nightly broadcasts.

A wonderful raconteur, Jax paints the British Columbia he loves in vivid colours and contrasts it with the terrains of both Germany and Israel, drawing on experiences as a wartime journalist. We may begin lying under a tree in Chilcotin County, admiring a bull moose, only to find ourselves transported back to another tree near Dieppe, France, hunting instead for German troops, and the beauty of both settings will haunt our memories equally. These stories that capture us with both his humour and his wisdom interrupt each other to establish connections that can only be seen in retrospect by someone whose love for nature and—much more difficult to achieve and sustain—for the strivings of the human animal has never wavered despite his immersion in the worst as well as the best moments. His memoir intersperses commentary with reminiscences of the beautiful Chilcotin wildernesses, while also introducing us to his family and friends and their stories, many of whom played memorable roles in Canadian history as well.

Each chapter informs and entertains the reader as we travel through time and across continents without leaving the comforting beauty of Timothy Meadow, Farwell Canyon and the numerous lakes and rivers that wind through Chilcotin country. The complementary beauties of mountains and Mozart's music, the lasting memory of manacles, and the frequent encounters with both moose and martinis chronicle not only the insights of Jax but also the maturation of his son Dan, known also as "the Tigger."

Born in Banff, Alberta, in 1916 and now living near Vancouver, British Columbia, since the early 1950s, Jax lived in Burma, India, and the United Kingdom in his youth and wandered through Spain, France and Germany before enlisting in his father's old regiment one week before the onset of World War II. Wounded in combat and evacuated to the UK, he transferred to the Canadian Army in 1942. Captured after the abortive Dieppe landing, he was a POW in Germany until late 1945. Having written as a Fleet Street print journalist before the war, after the war he shifted his perspective to Toronto, where he wrote for *Saturday Night Magazine* before becoming the news editor of radio station CKEY. Next he spent time with broadcast news, the radio news subsidiary of the *Canadian Press,* and then joined the editorial staff of the *Albertan* in Calgary, Alberta. Returning to radio, Jax eventually settled at CKWX in Vancouver, creating a signature newscast, "This Happened Today," broadcast at 6 and 10 p.m. each weeknight. His many careers included journalist, broadcaster, newsman, television actor ("Magistrate's Court"), investigative news reporter and talk-show host. On hand for such big news events as the raising of the Berlin Wall and the six-day Israeli War, Jax offered incisive and entertaining commentaries nightly. In these memoirs, similar commentaries alternate with quieter moments that reflect his abiding love for the Canadian wilderness. Enjoy the ride!

Dr. Thelma Richard, Professor Emerita
Arizona State University, Tempe

TABLE OF CONTENTS

Chapter Titles and List of Illustrations

CHAPTER 1
INITIAL RETROSPECTIVE

It was a magnificent early fall day. The sun was pleasantly warm. A few white clouds, typical of those in Chilcotin country, drifted across the otherwise clear sky in the west over the Coast Range. I was in my favourite position, sitting with my back against a tree after having walked about five miles from where we were camped. I had an uninterrupted view of the full mile or so length of the meadow as well as across its four-hundred-yard width and into the trees on the other side. One of the many branches of Brittany Creek meandered snake-like through the middle of the meadow to feed into a small lake at Far Meadow and my camp. The gentle breeze that moved the clouds slowly across the sky stirred and swayed the meadow grass very slightly.

I was about to fill and light my pipe when I saw the bull moose step out of the timber on the far side of the meadow and a couple of hundred yards to the west. His backside was hidden by a clump of willow. He wasn't feeding. He raised his head to test the breeze, but since I was downwind of him, there was no chance he'd know of my presence unless I made a sudden move. I eased gently back behind the spruce and raised my rifle to study him through the scope. He was about four years I reckoned and appeared to be in fine shape, since the rut was about to begin and either he'd already started collecting a harem of cows or was about to begin that process. I couldn't see any other animals in the timber behind him, but that didn't necessarily mean he had not started collecting females by which to do his male duty.

I was about to shoot, but then I thought, *What the hell? Why deprive him of the joy of impregnating at least one cow? And if I do shoot I'll have a devil of a time getting him across that creek even after I've skinned, cleaned and quartered him.* The other problem would be trying to get the Jimmy and trailer to this particular spot. The clumps of grass and willow made it impossible to get close enough to winch the animal across the creek, and I had no great desire to pack quarters of moose across the creek and the mile or so it would be necessary to carry those quarters to the closest place I could safely drive the Jimmy and trailer.

My son, best friend and longtime hunting and fishing partner for the last twenty years wouldn't be joining me back at my camp until the next day. Without his help I knew I'd have nothing but trouble trying to get fourteen or fifteen hundred pounds of butchered moose to where I could comfortably truck it back to camp, so I again said to myself, *What the hell?* I laid down my rifle, leaned back against the tree and watched as the young bull walked to a bend in the creek to drink. I lighted my pipe, and my idle thoughts drifted idly back to another place and another time some forty years before, when I was also sitting with my back to a tree....

* * *

It was August 19, 1942. The place, the cliffs to the east of the French coastal town, Dieppe. It too was a pleasantly warm afternoon. In the wood on top of the cliffs at that point, it was quiet. To the west, over and around Dieppe itself, there was still some firing, but it was now quite obvious the raid had failed. There were no more than a dozen of us in that wood. We were the only ones of the waves of men from the Fourth Brigade of the Canadian Second Division who'd managed to make it to the cliff top. We were awaiting nightfall and the slim possibility that some, if not all, of us could sneak out from that wooded area under cover of darkness and try to make contact with members of the French underground. That, or a much more likely probability of being ferreted out by German troops mopping up after, what turned out to be for us, a disastrous day.

Our colonel, Doug Catto, was one who'd made it to the cliff top. He had just made the round of those of us selected to set up a small defensive circle. Between us, we had a few rounds of rifle and Tommy gun ammunition, some grenades and one Bren gun. Catto told each of us we could make the choice of trying to break out on our own after dark, assuming by that time the enemy hadn't winkled us out, or await capture. There was a further possibility. We could fight it out, but Catto decided against it. He figured we'd taken enough of a mauling since we landed about twelve hours earlier as dawn was breaking. It was now obvious the Germans had advance knowledge of our coming. Indeed, some time much later we learned they had greatly reinforced their units in and around Dieppe.

Those of our small band on the cliff top who decided to turn it in, Catto advised they bury the ammunition, remove and bury weapon bolts and, those who had 'em, bury their commando knives. This latter was necessary because the Germans were known to deal roughly with what they called *die Kommando Spezial truppen* whom they, the Germans, considered to be "gangsters." Since I was one who had taken part in such hit-and-run raids prior to the Dieppe debacle and carried a knife, I decided to bury that weapon but hang on to my Tommy gun and try to break away on my own once darkness fell. Having made that decision, I settled back against the tree and began considering my chances. It looked very much as if it would be my last raid on German-occupied France, although if I could have subsequently made contact with the Maquis and was able to make it back to Britain eventually, I had hoped to take the SAS (Special Air Service) course I'd put in for prior to the Dieppe raid.

As it turned out, I didn't get back to Britain until the end of the war! But that afternoon, I didn't dream I'd be spending those next years behind barbed wire. Nor did I, sitting back to tree, weapon loaded and to hand, awaiting sound or sight of field grey-clad enemy troops, think that decades later I'd be sitting with my back against another tree, another weapon loaded and to hand, deciding whether to shoot a bull moose.

* * *

The years between have treated me most fortunately, and coming back to the present that afternoon in a Chilcotin meadow, I reflected on how mountains, Mozart, manacles, moose and martinis have figured throughout much of my life.

You recall I mentioned earlier that the Germans considered commando troops as gangsters, or if you will, silent killers on raids into enemy-held territory. Another item of individual equipment on those raids was a length of rope, to the ends of which were attached small pieces of wood known as toggles. These were used in a variety of ways; secured together for cliff and/or tree climbing, and when the occasion arose, for tying prisoners. It was this latter practise that produced an international incident out of the Dieppe raid that came back to haunt us weeks and months later.

When our troops hit the beaches on either side of Dieppe that morning in August of '42, a small number of Germans were taken prisoner. To make sure they didn't disappear from the beaches as our lads moved inland, the prisoners were tied in the traditional fashion of hit-and-run raiding parties. That is, they were made to lie on their stomachs, a looped rope was placed around their necks, and they were then made to bend back their legs with their hands behind their backs. The rope was then wrapped around their wrists and feet, effectively hogtying them. If they struggled, they stood the chance of strangling themselves. Otherwise they lay there until they could be released by their own troops after the particular raid ended or be taken back by the raiding party.

While the battle on Dieppe's beaches raged that day, some of the German prisoners who'd been tied and left in that fashion as our troops moved inland were caught by incoming tides and drowned. That subsequently raised merry hell between German authorities and the British and Canadian governments. Some weeks after we were lodged in German prison camps, we Canadians who'd taken part in the Dieppe show were manacled. Each morning German guards marched in, carrying bundles of handcuffs. They'd line us up and cuff our hands in front. We were supposed to keep the cuffs on until the evening. However, that didn't last. As soon as the guards left in the morning, with judicious use of a fork or knife we'd pry back the spring in each cuff and remove the "bracelets." Minutes before the guards returned in the evening, we'd put our cuffs back on our wrists, and the guards would go through the process of releasing us, using specially made keys. It wasn't too long, however, before the guards themselves became thoroughly sick and tired of the whole damned exercise. So when they came in mornings, they'd simply leave the requisite number of sets of handcuffs on tables in our huts and return to pick 'em up again in the evening.

The next chapter in this farcical procedure came when the guards realised that each evening they were collecting a lesser number of handcuffs than they'd distributed that morning. That was because we POWs were hiding 'em as souvenirs—not only Canadians but other prisoners also. After some months the Germans apparently came to the realisation the exercise was a complete waste of time, to say nothing of the metal needed to make an ever-increasing number of handcuffs, and they stopped the daily distribution. Remarkably, though, whenever a German brass hat visited a particular camp, they'd manacle a certain number of us, undoubtedly to make it look good!

Thus the manacles portion of the title of these verbal wanderings.

As for mountains, I was born surrounded by 'em. I was an army brat. My father had been seconded to the Canadian forces from the British army during the First World War. My mother was with him when he came to this country, and I made my appearance while they were on a brief holiday in Banff. Within a few months, however, he was returned to the British army and was ordered to duty in the Far East, specifically Burma, for a couple of years. By that time the supposed "war to end all wars" ended, and we moved to India and the Northwest Frontier. Thus by the time I was old enough to sit up and take notice, so to speak, I came to know the Himalayas.

Many years later as a fledgling newsman, I spent time in areas dominated by the Swiss, Austrian and Bavarian Alps. There was even a brief spell in the late thirties when I found myself in the shadow of the Pyrenees during the Spanish Civil War. It wasn't until 1949, while working on a Calgary daily, *The Albertan*, that I completed my first world circuit. I travelled one weekend to Banff from the Stampede City and began to feel kinship with the title and theme of that aria, "Ai Nostri Monti" ("Home to My Mountains"), from the last act of Verdi's *Il Travatore*. Even so, it wasn't until I came the very next year to settle in this most beautiful of all provinces, British Columbia, and some years after that when I started hunting in Chilcotin country, that I felt I was truly home to *my* mountains, the Coast and Chilcotin ranges.

Once you pass through the spectacular gorge through which runs the mighty and, as W.A.C. Bennett called it, the muddy Fraser, a few miles west of Williams Lake, you travel hundreds of feet up and out onto a vast plateau. Miles away to the west can be seen the Coast and Chilcotin ranges. They contain the highest mountain in British Columbia, indeed the highest in Canada outside the border area of Yukon and Alaska. Mount Waddington rises 13,177 feet and is said to dominate more than four hundred square miles of Arctic-like ice and rock well above tree line.

Other peaks, not nearly so high but close in their majestic splendour, carry names as spectacular as the country from which they rise: Tsuniah, Tatlow and Konni, among others. Below are lakes and rivers with names that reflect the ancient native heritage of the region: Chilcotin, Chilco, Taseko, Tatloyoko, Tatla, Chaunigan and dozens more, some unnamed on most maps, but undoubtedly known to local residents.

This is the area and these the mountains, rivers and lakes to which I have returned almost every year since the late 1950s, except for the occasional journey into Peace River and Omineca country, to hunt and fish.

My love of the music of Wolfgang Amadeus Mozart started long before the fairly recent movie loosely based on his all-too-short life and turbulent times. My mother, one of the Fraser clan, who spoke in the soft tones of her native Invernesshire, used to subject us as children to what she called a "music bath" many an evening. Together with the music recitals she would read to us from the life stories of the great composers.

Of the major arts, music, painting and literature, I have always had the greatest reverence for those who composed music. To my way of thinking, painters have before them the subject from which to put a likeness on canvas. The writer and poet to some extent have similar prototypes. The composer, however, must transpose and translate sound literally from thin air, sound that can in turn be documented and recorded for all time.

Mozart's compositions are most eclectic indeed. Much of his work seems to reflect his own delight in poking fun at established authority and the traditions of his day, a classic case in point being "The Magic Flute." As over the years I've been privileged to give forth in print, on the air and on camera with my opinions on all manner of issues. I too was often accused of being eclectic in my political ideas and no respecter of persons in high office or in public life generally.

I've also long believed that much of Mozart's music, like Nature itself, is no respecter of the human voice and hand, as I'm sure many operatic singers as well as accomplished pianists would attest to, having tried to master the composer's wide and taxing range of arpeggios and scales. At the same time, many of his compositions seem emblematic of the soaring majesty of the mountains; the swift flow of wild rivers; the calm, pristine beauty of high lakes; the broad loneliness of wilderness meadows and silences one can literally feel. In this regard, his last symphony, the "Jupiter," springs to mind, as does the "Gloria in Excelsis Deo," reflective of God's handiwork in all those things.

What does Mozart have to do with fishing and hunting in the Chilcotin or elsewhere? It is my practise to take with me, on my wilderness trips, tape recorder and cassettes of my favourite music, Mozart being predominant. Not only have my partners on these trips been subjected to symphonies, concerti, arias and sacred choruses many evenings after dinner, but undoubtedly so also have the animals in the high country. Fortified with a brace of martinis, replete with good food in the comfortable warmth of a camper or cabin (even on occasion in a tent), nothing soothes mind and body more than a wilderness concert.

Now for martinis. As earlier indicated, these are imbibed at the end of the day, rarely to excess but more as a relaxant prior to the evening meal. No one throughout the years I've made these trips has yet complained about my wilderness culinary abilities. (Whether out of respect for those abilities, regard for my advancing years, because they'd rather eat than cook or simply because the evening's libation has lulled them, I've never discovered.) The lone exception to the martini tradition is my earlier-mentioned best friend, hunting and fishing partner, my son Dan. Long ago named by me the Tigger, arising from his childhood reading of *Winnie the Pooh* tales, he is a confirmed but moderate beer drinker. Any brand. Which reinforces the contention there is in fact no accounting for taste!

It has been said of the martini, gin or vodka, that it can be likened to a woman's breasts. One is not enough and three are too many. My usual intake is two, although on occasion I've been known to indulge in a third. But for the life of me I cannot see the connection, even though I have throughout my adult life been what might be correctly considered a devoted student of "mammarian architecture."

For years I've called a martini "clear olive soup." On one occasion, that led to an amusing incident at my then favourite Vancouver dining establishment, Nat Bailey's original White Spot on South Granville Street. The bartender made excellent martinis. One day when a colleague and I went to lunch, we were greeted by the hostess with the story. The previous day, two dear old ladies, regular White Spot customers, had informed the waitress they wished to start their meal with clear olive soup. When the waitress looked somewhat puzzled, they became indignant, telling her that only a few days before they had distinctly heard "Jax" on the air telling people how good was the White Spot clear olive soup! After the hostess explained, the ladies decided against trying said "soup." Whether they ever listened to my daily verbal wanderings thereafter, I never knew.

Fall Storm Sky—Shot by son, Dan Jacques

CHAPTER 2
HOHENFELS JOY JUICE

During the last two decades of the nineteenth century, the prairie towns of Canada were beginning to look as if they would become permanent centres of population and not mere wayside camps for railroad workers and adventurers from eastern Canada, the U.S. and many parts of Europe. The main methods of relaxation for these men in those towns were whoring and boozing. The two went hand in hand simply because the brothels, which were often in business long before hotels and churches, let alone schools and hospitals, were established and were also distribution places for liquor.

When the moral reformers and temperance crusaders in those growing population centres got into full stride, they aimed their slings and arrows of outrage at what they called the social evil of prostitution and that other instrument of the Devil, "distilled damnation"—booze.

A great number of the immigrants who helped establish Canada's prairie population centres were from central and eastern Europe. They brought with them not only their muscle power and dogged determination to make it in their new country but also centuries' old knowledge of how to make booze and how to add to or expand upon the strength of distilled concoctions already in existence in Canada. None of the newcomers to this country were more adept at producing very potent "distilled damnation" than the Scots. After all, they'd been brewing their own distillations long before Canada became…Canada. In retrospect, therefore, it is not surprising that my first experience with the end product of home brew came at the hands of a Scot. This occurred also long before I discovered "olive soup."

It was a few months after the Dieppe debacle. With nightfall that day and date (August 19, 1942), I made my bid to contact French underground forces. But before I was able to do that, I was picked up by roving German troops and, having sustained a slight head wound, was shipped to hospital in Rouen. It was there, incidentally, that I first met one of the two men later awarded the Victoria Cross for their part in the Dieppe raid, Colonel Cec Merritt. The other VC, Padre John Foote, I had known previously since he was the Fourth Canadian Brigade padre. I didn't meet Merritt again after the Germans shipped us from Rouen to various camps inside the Third Reich but had re-established contact after coming to Vancouver. Foote and I came to know each other when we both wound up in a camp in Bavaria not far from a small village named Hohenfels—the very same camp where I learned to make and tasted my first home brew at the hands of the earlier-mentioned Scot.

The Hohenfels camp was established in the main for Non-Commissioned and Warrant Officers from all parts of the British Commonwealth, the United Kingdom, Canada, Australia, New Zealand, South Africa and Rhodesia. There were even one or two Yanks who had been shot down while flying with either the RCAF or what was known as the Eagle Squadron, a unit of Americans flying with the Royal Air Force before the U.S. got into the war. John Foote was of course a commissioned officer, but instead of going to a camp for officers, he'd coerced the Germans into allowing him to go to a camp for other ranks, Hohenfels, because he felt he could do more of the Almighty's work with the larger flock of men in that camp than at an *Oflag* or officers' camp.

Foote was Presbyterian, as was I (another legacy from my dear old Mum). Even so, the padre and I got into some hot and heavy arguments about the existence of God and religion generally during our Hohenfels stay. So hot and heavy, in fact, that at one point he told me, "Jax, much more of this and I swear you'll drive me to booze." I never saw John again after I was moved from Hohenfels, but a year or so after we returned to Canada I read with amusement a report that John Foote had been appointed a member of the Ontario Liquor Commission!

Meantime, the Scot who introduced me to home brewing hailed from the Shetland Isles. He had that soft, lilting manner of speech common to Scottish Islanders (as opposed to Highlanders) and would refer for example to "Shermans" and "Shaps" rather than Germans and Japs. In civilian life he'd been a blacksmith. He was a stocky, powerfully built fellow and, remarkably, he neither smoked nor drank. But he certainly knew how to make a potent brew. In fact I'm sure those islanders, if not born with that skill, learn it in their childhood.

The ingredients for brewing Hohenfels joy juice were, in the main, readily available in Canadian Red Cross parcels, something I'm quite sure officials of that honourable organization never in their wildest imaginings figured. Canadian Red Cross parcels were the most popular with the majority of POWs, and not, I hasten to add, because they contained home-brew ingredients: dried fruits, such as prunes and raisins, and sugar. The other main ingredient, yeast, we got from our own camp cooks and bakers who in turn bribed guards for it, using the universal means of exchange in all POW camps, cigarettes. Particularly when they were away from the fighting front, German troops were rationed to ten cigarettes or two small cigars per day. Thus cigarettes were pretty near worth their weight in gold to us and them.

The Shetlander who made his name and fame as the Hohenfels master distiller used to instruct us, for the flat rate of five hundred cigarettes, in how to lay down a brew. The earlier-mentioned staple ingredients were mixed into a mash in buckets, large zinc bowls, and even, in some cases where a deal could be made with guards with the requisite number of cigarettes, in a wooden cask or hogshead. With the passage of years, I've forgotten precise amounts and time requirements, but I do recall that the first brew we made in the hut I shared at that time, made up of a dozen of us, didn't stay overlong in the cask.

We decided to get the still operational one cold, clear Sunday in February 1943. There was snow outside to a depth of five or six inches, so we had a ready-made cooling system. We put dollops of the mash into a gallon zinc jug, supplied to each hut by the Germans for carrying water and brewing tea and coffee (the latter from Red Cross parcels). An airtight lid was made for the jug from a flattened Klim powdered milk can, still another Canadian parcel item. A piece of copper pipe ran from the lid and was passed through a standup bath-sized container filled with snow and ice. The jug of mash was already on the stove, and before many hours passed, the distillation was dripping gently into a series of litre bottles. By day's end we'd taken off about a dozen litres of what can only be described as clear liquid dynamite. We stacked the bottles under bunks alongside the walls of our hut before turning in for the night.

However, it wasn't long after that before one of our group, an Aussie from the King's Cross area of Sydney who'd been captured in North Africa, called out a familiar Aussie greeting: "Jax, you baaastard," (the broad "a" is never more pronounced than by Aussies in that particular epithet!), "let's try a shot of that firewater."

We did. Not just one shot. Over the next couple of hours we opened and drained three or four bottles. We were making such a racket in our hut, which was only a few yards from the main gate of the camp, that a couple of guards were sent in to find out what was afoot. They quickly discovered not only what was happening but also what was the cause…by themselves sampling said cause. Shortly thereafter, they were joining us in raucous song, including that favourite on both sides in the European war, "Lili Marlene." I don't know what happened to those guards. I do know that I wandered out into the night and the snow for a walk and fell fast asleep in the snow-covered playing field at the top end of the camp. Never even experienced a hangover next day. In later conversation with the Shetlander, he explained that was not unusual, given the fact we'd been drinking pure booze unadulterated by colour additives and soft drink mix.

The Germans confiscated our still, but not what was left of the end product. That had been distributed to other nearby huts. It was only a matter of days, however, before we were back fully in business, as were other groups in other huts throughout the camp, thanks as always to the non-drinking, non-smoking Shetlander and those priceless Canadian Red Cross parcel ingredients.

More than a year later, in another camp in Pomerania on the German Baltic coast, I was introduced to a very different item of "distilled damnation"! Early in 1944 some faceless bureaucrat in the higher echelons of German government decreed that Canadian prisoners of war deserved special treatment. At the time there were but a handful of us in Hohenfels, the majority of our fellows taken at Dieppe having been shipped from France directly to a camp in Poland already containing hundreds of Brits. At that juncture of our time behind barbed wire, we were already familiar enough with German terminology to realise special treatment could mean anything, and we were therefore not exactly overjoyed at the prospect of being shipped to a "special treatment" camp. It turned out, however, that about that time the first German "repats" had been returned to their Fatherland from prison camps in Canada. Repats were prisoners who'd been severely wounded or were paraplegics and quadriplegics. Such repatriation involved only Western Allied POWs. The International Red Cross and other protective power organizations had no contact with Russian prisoners in German hands simply because Stalin had decreed that any of his troops taken prisoner were automatically deprived of Russian citizenship, were to be considered cowards in the face of the enemy, and if returned to their Soviet motherland, would be summarily executed—a little-known fact that has rarely been publicized since the end of that war.

Repatriated German prisoners, particularly those who'd been in Canada, were lavish in their praise of the treatment they'd generally received over here, which brought about the "special treatment" decree apropos Canadian prisoners in Germany. Even so, Stalag 11 D at Stargard in Pomerania, not unexpectedly, was certainly not a holiday camp. If anything, the "special treatment" was a propaganda move by the Germans, if not also an attempt to split Commonwealth prisoners, very much along the lines of one of the first questions our captors threw at us shortly after we were nabbed: "Where are 'die Tommies' (the English)? Are they using you Canadians to fight their war?" Of course, that didn't work any more than did the "special treatment" ploy.

Practically all of us taken at Dieppe, some fifteen hundred other ranks, were gathered together at Stargard. For those whose history is either rusty or non-existent in this context, of the five thousand Canadian troops who embarked from southern English points for Dieppe that August day, little more than 3,500 landed. Of those, less than a thousand managed to make it back to Britain at day's end. Almost a thousand officers and men were killed. The remainder, most wounded to some degree, were captured.

The Stargard camp was much larger than that at Hohenfels. There were a number of separate compounds housing Canadian, French, Yugoslav and Russian prisoners. A couple of times a week during the spring and summer of that year, 1944, the Germans allowed a couple of dozen of us "*Kanadier Schwein,*" along with an equal number of prisoners of the other nationalities to travel by train under escort about twenty miles outside the town of Stargard into a forested area. There we were to dig out and split tree stumps as fuel for stove and kitchen fires in the camp. Very little work was ever accomplished on those trips. The guards, as was more often than not the case, were mostly frontline troops awaiting re-assignment to their old units following furlough from the front or recovering from wounds. Furthermore, by that stage of the war, the majority had served on the east (Russian) front and were not particularly anxious to return to that deadly theatre. Almost every one of 'em knew, and many readily admitted, they'd already lost the war. So all in all, they were just as willing to goof off as were we, especially when it came to physical labour. The result was that, if our woods-work parties managed to uproot and split more than three or four stumps a day, we and the guards figured we were working too hard. So we sat around, usually in my favourite position, backs to trees, and indulged in the age-old soldierly pastime, bullshitting.

On one such day, a group of Russian officer prisoners came out with us. The Canadian contingent at Stargard did have fellows of both Russian and Ukrainian extraction, but on that particular day none of these was on the stump-splitting party, which resulted in Russkies and Canadians conversing in…German!

When we quit what little work we had been doing for the lunch break, the Russians produced a demijohn, uncorked it, and after each of them had taken a swig, they passed it to the guards. I happened to be chatting with the NCO in charge of the guard detachment and was invited to take a swallow. Looking forward to a Russian prisoner version of vodka or a reasonable facsimile thereof, I took a deep draught. For the next few seconds I thought I'd wind up in the top of the nearby trees. I could scarcely get my breath for all of three or four minutes. Through eyes brimming with tears, I saw guards, Russians and even my Canadian confreres laughing uncontrollably as I slowly recovered composure and equilibrium. When I was able to return to a near normal state, I learned I'd taken a healthy swig of rubbing alcohol, which the Russians had "liberated" from the camp hospital.

I swear by all that's holy, those Russians must have had leather-lined stomachs. Either that or, given their bleak future in view of Stalin's murderous edict concerning prisoners, they figured they may as well drown their sorrows in alcohol of any kind.

* * *

A couple of years later, after returning to Canada, I was in Toronto and ran into an old regimental comrade, Elmer Kyle (Tony) Anthony. Among other claims to fame Tony was at the start of that war the youngest sergeant major in the Canadian army at twenty-nine, having transferred from the permanent force Royal Canadian Regiment to the regiment I subsequently joined and where I met him, the Royal Regiment of Canada. He was back on civvy street also and was living on Centre Island across the harbour from Toronto proper. He and his wife, Mae, were what were known as "year round island residents" in those days—year round in that they lived there permanently, whereas a majority of people who lived on the island did so only during the summer.

At that time also, there was only one beer parlour on the island, and it served only beer. There were no legal liquor outlets, the nearest being across in the city. During winter months, particularly when ice formed on the harbour, the regular ferries didn't operate. Instead there were a number of runs between the city and the island by ice-breaking tugs. Permanent island residents who worked in Toronto or who wished to go there to shop or whatever rode the tugs to and fro. However, those vessels ran hourly only between seven *ayem* and eleven *pee em*. People who missed the last tug at night were stranded in the city or on the other side. Anthony and I realised here was a great opportunity to make our name and fame, if not also our fortune, by going into the booze business, especially given the fact that island residents who missed tug sailings, if they hadn't gotten in a stock of hard liquor on Toronto trips, were S.O.L. for booze on the island itself. Ergo, we set up a still, using my then much clearer recollection of how to do that from the Hohenfels joy juice experience. For a few weeks, we did a roaring trade. Until one cold, clear night in February of 1947. A detachment of Queen's Cowboys (RCMP) stationed at Hanlan's Point two or three miles to the west of us sniffed the air and very soon thereafter were able to pinpoint our illicit operations. They were extremely kind to us, probably because we were war vets and ex-POWs, so instead of charging us, they quietly confiscated our still and let us off with a warning. So ended our short but happy and most successful venture into the booze business. A pity really, since we were providing what many permanent island residents thought was a vital public service at very reasonable rates and were not adding into our prices any governmental tax bite!

* * *

In later years, the nearest I have come to tasting a libation as smooth, to say nothing of being as powerful, as those from Hohenfels or Centre Island was when I experienced a Schuk Shake. Now, although much of this province lies on or near an earthquake zone, the most prominent being the San Andreas Fault, the Schuk Shake has nothing whatsoever to do with earthquakes or movement of landmass. Although after imbibing a Schuk Shake, I've known people to claim the land does move.

In the years I've hunted and fished in Chilcotin country, I've come to know a number of people up there, prominent among them the Schuk clan. The patriarch, Joe Schuk, settled there from his birthplace in Saskatchewan in the thirties. He married a born and bred Chilcotin lass, Kate, and started a cattle ranch, still in operation in the Tatloyoko Valley. Two of Joe's offspring, Cal and Cliff, now run their own spreads a few miles away.

Until the late forties, Kate and Joe, occasionally with a neighbour or two, drove cattle for sale on horseback the almost two hundred miles from their home ranch to Williams Lake, a journey that then took three weeks to a month. Nowadays cattle are trucked that distance over greatly improved roads. I first met Joe years ago when a partner and I were camped alongside one of the many unnamed small lakes up there. We had a skinned and quartered moose hanging in the trees and were just finishing lunch when Joe, out looking for stray cattle, rode in to pass the time of day. After joining us in a glass of conviviality, he went on his way. In subsequent years, those who've accompanied me on my Chilcotin trips, including my son, have often enjoyed the unstinting hospitality of, and have raised many a glass with, Joe, Cal and Cliff and their ladies.

It was Cal and Cliff who invented the Schuk Shake. They'd been spending a few days in one of their line cabins preparing to winter some of their cattle at a spot known as Timothy Meadow. One evening, they were contemplating what was left of a bottle of rye and another containing two or three measures of apricot brandy. While both have since laid claim to discovering the solution to their problem of that evening, I tend to believe it was the older, more phlegmatic Cal who hit on the ideal solution. Believing a combination of rye and apricot brandy alone might do more harm than good, he decided to add an equal measure of the pure, cold water from a spring on the property, which, in turn, emanates from the ubiquitous Brittany Creek. Thus the Schuk Shake. I can personally attest to its incredible smoothness and most pleasant taste as well as its dreamless sleep-inducing qualities. One evening when a couple of hunting partners and I had dined with Cliff Schuk, we were treated to our first Shakes before leaving his place to head down to the Chilko River, about five miles away.

To this day not one of us can recall any part of that five-mile jaunt. We did make it without mishap, and next morning found ourselves exactly where we wished to be on the far side of the river. Obviously we had slept deeply and well. And as further testament to the insulating qualities of the Schuk Shake, all three of us the following morning strip washed in the river and that, in late October in a glacier-fed river, is not for the faint of heart.

In a subsequent broadcast on my return to the coast, I told the story of the Schuk Shake and received numerous calls and letters asking for the ingredients. One lady wrote that she and her husband were camping near Fort St. John when they heard that particular broadcast. After buying rye and apricot brandy from a Fort St. John liquor store, they added the required amount of water from that part of the province. They claimed it made a most pleasant nightcap. Somehow though, I doubt a Schuk Shake could be quite the same without Chilcotin rivers or Brittany Creek water. As they used to say in a commercial promoting a particular Washington State beer, I'm sure "it's the water!"

Former Hohenfels POW camp.
Note base of former watch tower left foreground

CHAPTER 3
SMOKEY'S CHRISTENING

It was while I was once more in my favourite position after walking a few miles then sitting, back to a spruce, smoking a pipe, that I first made indirect contact with Cliff Schuk. I was on a hillside looking down over a wild meadow through which ran—what else but—the meandering Brittany Creek. If you study a forestry map of the country south and east of the Chilcotin River as it flows out of the Coast Range near the place known as Henry's Crossing (named after a now departed Chilcotin chief named Henry Lulu), you will see numerous times the title "Brittany Creek." At one point it runs into and out of a horseshoe-shaped lake also named Brittany.

On the day I speak of in this chapter, looking down on that portion of the creek and the meadow through which it flowed, I was looking at what for me then was new country. Studying the scene below, I noticed what looked like a little used logging road where it petered out into the meadow itself. I climbed down to the road and after following it for about a mile found an old, but clearly still used, cabin. A couple of full hay corrals stood nearby. There was no one around, but the cabin door was not locked, so I walked in. It was a two-room structure, the first part a kind of storeroom filled with farm equipment and old furniture. The rear section of the cabin was comfortably furnished with table, chairs and a couple of bedsprings, on which were rolled up mattresses. Suspended from the roof were blankets and pillows. In one corner, also suspended from the roof timbers by two by fours, hung a well-used chuckwagon food box. Cupboards around the walls were filled with dishes and cutlery. Pots and pans hung from nails on the walls. In the centre of the room stood an ancient four-burner wood stove complete with oven and water container. The stove was quite cold. On the table under a small rear window was a child's exercise book. I leafed through it and discovered it was a kind of diary. The entries told of someone having spent much of the previous winter there, feeding cattle and trapping. Each day's temperature and snow depth was recorded. The diary revealed that the previous Christmas snow had fallen to a depth of two feet and the mercury had dipped and stayed at fifty below on what I've always contended to be the understandable scale, Fahrenheit. One entry read: "Father came over Christmas day by horse and cutter to spend a few days." I learned much later when I got to know the Schuk clan better, that the round trip from Joe Schuk's home ranch to Timothy Meadow and return was more than fifty miles.

Another entry read: "lost a calf to a cougar." A few days later, "tracked and shot the cougar." Some entries told of cattle being taken by wolves and of trapping and shooting wolves.

What greatly intrigued me about the diary was that in these days with all our electrically powered gadgets on hand to make our urban and suburban lives so easy, up there, less than four hundred miles due north of BC's major population centre, life went on as it had done for decades. This was by no means an isolated case. There are still sturdy, independent folk, Indian and white, in many areas of this vast province who continue to live out their lives in such remote places. Indeed, except for the occasional trip out to Williams Lake, and even rarer trips to the Lower Mainland, they seem much to prefer it that way. On one of his brief visits to our Lower Mainland home, Cliff Schuk told us that, while he enjoyed watching television and using the telephone, after a few days down here he liked to get back because "it soon gets boring here"!

On that first visit to the Timothy Meadow cabin, I borrowed the diary, which I later learned had been written by Cliff. I brought it back to what many of us still call civilization. After photocopying the contents, prior to airing some of the more general entries in future broadcasts, I sent it back with a covering note to the NCO in charge of the Alexis Creek RCMP detachment for subsequent return to the writer.

In the years since, and with the blessing of Cliff, older brother Cal and clan patriarch Joe, I've spent many days and nights using that cabin as a base on hunting trips. So also has the Tigger, who now knows almost all of that part of Chilcotin country as well as, if not better than, myself.

On one of those later trips, my son and a young Lower Mainland police officer came along. During that, for him, first-ever hunting trip, the officer inadvertently came to be known as Smokey. His given name was Doug Johnson. The sobriquet Smokey, however, had nothing to do with his profession, even though during his early years of police work he had done his share of traffic patrols. Those familiar with the language of CB users will know that Smokey is the usual reference to police when one long-haul trucker is alerting others to the presence of highway patrol vehicles in the vicinity. Doug, however, came by the name in an entirely different context.

At this point I should explain that prior to his time with the Lower Mainland department he was then with, Johnson had had a half dozen years with the Calgary department. During those years, he built himself a good reputation as a hard-working and effective copper. However, his biggest claim to fame while on that force came one Sunday morning while he was on motorcycle patrol. As he told the story to me, he had gone into a restaurant that was regularly patronized by officers on patrol to have breakfast. Wearing helmet, sunglasses, gauntlets, breeches and high boots, he clearly cut a macho, if not also, to the young things in the establishment, romantic figure. He sat down at a table near the entrance,,, from where he could survey the whole place and draw the eyes and attention of the covey of young women customers as well as the waitresses.

"I enjoyed a leisurely meal, all the while basking in the admiring and not always shy glances of the girls," he continued with a smile. "At the end of my breakfast, I picked up my helmet and gloves from the floor beside me and, with sunglasses in t'other hand, rose to leave." He was obviously as determined to make as grand an exit as his entrance. It didn't quite turn out that way.

In his words, "I suddenly went arse over tip, flat on my back, helmet and gloves sliding one way, sunglasses the other." It seems his shoulder harness and belt caught the back of his chair.

As he picked himself up, there was a painful silence throughout the establishment; but as he turned to walk out, dignity and ego badly shattered, first one young woman and then others started to giggle. "When I swung astride my motorcycle, I could hear the giggles turn into peals of laughter," he admitted. "I didn't leave the Calgary force for another few months, but," he added, "I never went near that place again."

Now, on this young man's first hunting trip, we reached Timothy Meadow late in the day. By the time we'd unloaded food, sleeping bags, guns, *etcetera* and the lamps were filled and lighted and water hauled in, it was fully dark. The Tigger had split wood, which Doug carried into the cabin and was piling by the stove. One of them started the fire as I prepared dinner, after having built and taste-tested the evening's batch of martinis for Doug and myself. Suddenly we noticed that the stove wasn't drawing all that well, and smoke kept drifting back into the cabin. It subsided somewhat while we were eating dinner but started again when I was heating water for the dishes.

Later as I washed dishes, wearing a pair of goggles the lad had brought with him (Lord knows why and I cannot recall where he got 'em nor for what particular purpose), the Tigger, not being too enthusiastic about washing dishes, was rummaging around outside. He found a bush carpentry-type ladder with which he climbed to the cabin roof to see if he could spot a bird or pack rat nest in the chimney, but the pipe was clear of any obstruction. Even so, very little smoke was getting out. We didn't stoke the stove that night, the cabin being warm enough as it was.

Being much more enthusiastic about hunting than chores like dishwashing, Dan was up and out soon after first light next morning exploring the surrounding country. An hour later he was back to report that, while he hadn't seen birds or animals, he had noticed fresh tracks crossing the road half a mile behind the cabin. He also said he'd heard some cracking in the timber in the area where he'd seen the tracks but hadn't gone to investigate further.

We had a light breakfast of bread and fruit, and shortly thereafter all three of us headed up the road to examine the tracks the Tigger had found. At the point where he'd heard the cracking and seen the tracks, I knew a moose had crossed down to the creek to drink and headed back into the timber. It was clear the tracks had been made that morning. I stationed Doug by a stand of young jack pine just off the road, while the Tigger and I moved along the road for a few yards then cut in and walked quietly and slowly for about a hundred yards more. To our left and about fifty yards above where Doug was stationed, I saw a tuft of grass moving behind a wind-felled log. There was hardly any breeze, and as I was about to move toward that spot, up stood the moose. It was the first the lad had ever seen in the timber, and his immediate reaction was a whispered, "Jeez, Dad, he's big!"

I couldn't see if the animal had a rack, nor could the Tigger, despite his spontaneous remark and inadvertent reference to gender. I should point out here I have never, nor will I ever, shoot a cow moose, even when the cow season is open. In some respects that's because, when Dan was much smaller before he ever made a trip into the timber with me, he would always say before I left, "Please, Dad, don't shoot the mums or the babies."

The moose we both saw that morning wasn't spooked by us when he stood. He turned leisurely and started trotting up the hill and away from where we were. But I still couldn't see a rack of antlers, simply because the angle at which the animal was moving made it impossible to tell, even using the rifle scope and no matter which way I moved, whether in fact it carried a rack. Not, that is, until the moose crested the hill. Only then did I catch the sunlight on the blades of a large rack. I started moving fast then, following the bull, but he was moving much faster. Although I followed him for a mile or more before losing sight of him, and throughout that time simply couldn't get a clear shot, I must admit I wasn't as concerned as I should have been. You see, I figured that, with Doug stationed directly below where the animal stood up, the young copper must surely have seen whether it was a bull or not.

Not until I saw the blades flash in the sun did I begin to wonder why the devil Doug hadn't shot. Here, after all, was a tall, healthy-looking young policeman with eight or nine years' experience in that profession and with the attendant knowledge of weapons and shooting. I'd stationed this young fellow a few yards from me that morning as I tried, and failed, to identify the sex of the moose, which was now most likely two or three miles away. When I returned from my fruitless chase, Doug was no longer where I'd told him to stand. But when Dan and I got back to the cabin, there he was, seated outside and still shaking.

I knew immediately what had happened. It strikes many fellows, and this strapping young copper was no exception. It is known as buck fever. The neophyte hunter is all keyed up when an animal appears. The adrenalin is pumping, the heart pounding, the animal squarely in his rifle sight and…he simply cannot shoot. Often he can't even move from that spot for quite a while, even after the animal has disappeared.

Doug had succumbed to buck fever even though, during his years in uniform—as is sometimes the case with policemen on patrol, particularly at night—he had more than once faced the most dangerous animal, an armed man bent on criminal intent, and he had come through that experience none the worse for it.

I have never experienced buck fever. Whether that has anything to do with my times in combat, I don't really know. I will also admit I've never been faced by a charging grizzly, although I have seen a bull moose in full charge. In Johnson's case, as with a number of men—even, on occasion, women—hunting big game for the first time, buck fever remains a largely inexplicable phenomenon. Interestingly, Doug accompanied me on a Chilcotin trip again the very next year, and although he didn't have to do the shooting, we did get a moose that time. A year or so after that, he left police work entirely. I've not seen nor heard from him since, but I did hear from one of his former departmental colleagues that he'd left the province and gone into stock-brokering down East somewhere. I do hope the bulls of the market place have been kinder to him than his first bull moose!

Later on the day that Doug saw his first bull moose, while I was preparing the evening meal and the martinis were being sipped, we discovered the cause of the previous evening's smoke episode. As I went to start the fire in the stove, the answer, as with so many problems in life, became quite clear. In his desire to pile wood as neatly as possible behind the stove the night before, Doug had accidentally jammed shut the lower damper. We never again suffered smoke problems in that, nor in any other, cabin. But ever since, Doug Johnson has been known to the Tigger and myself as Smokey.

The denouement to the full day's events, however, came after dinner that evening when the Tigger, just before falling asleep and obviously having gone over those events in his mind, suddenly called to me: "What were you waiting to do this morning, Dad? Take pictures?"

Timothy Meadow cabin (not well favored by Andrea & Lila)

CHAPTER 4
ROCKS, ROCKS AND MORE ROCKS

Rocks are a blessing in the high country, especially when one is crossing a creek or a black and oozy mud hole in a vehicle. By the same token, rocks have been known to wreck, even rip out, vehicle transmissions; smash axles; and hole fuel tanks when people drive into Chilcotin country without the right added equipment of steel plate under both fuel tank and transmission—or as has been known to happen, when people drive without regard for terrain and commonsense. Rocks are also the cause of lesser vehicle damage, and it's not uncommon to see RCMP vehicles with cracked windshields and shattered headlights. Indeed, those pertinent sections of the Motor Vehicle Act have as much efficacy up in that country as FACs (Firearms Acquisition Certificates). For most Chilcotin residents, FACs had even less usefulness than toilet paper, although they could be used for fire starters. None are more aware of this, and act accordingly, than the Queen's Cowboy members in such remote areas.

I recall one evening in particular when I was accompanied, for his first trip into the Chilcotin, by a longtime, former West Coast unionist by the name of Alf Poole. This was also one of my son's early trips. Poole was then the head honcho of what I've long called the "Seafairies": the SIU, Seafarers' International Union on the West Coast. He, in turn, was known as the Ancient Mariner, a sobriquet of which he was not overly fond, given that he was remarkably shy about admitting to his correct age. On his first hunting trip with me, we had spent much of the afternoon of our first day out in Williams

Lake. I had earlier arranged to interview at his office in that town with Howard Mitchell, a longtime game biologist and conservation officer best known for his years of work with California Bighorn sheep. Mitchell, in fact, actually re-seeded the Farwell Canyon area a few miles south of Riske Creek with those animals. Prior to his work in this regard, California Bighorns were near extinction in this province and had been pretty well wiped out in the American state of that name. More than a decade after he took on this Herculean task, during which he had to battle ranchers in that area as well as entrenched bureaucrats even in his own department of provincial government, Mitchell brought the Bighorn count in Farwell to some three hundred animals. Thereafter, and with his departmental colleagues finally on side, he was able to send animals to the Kootenays and down into the U.S., including California. Today California Bighorn sheep are no longer on the endangered species list in this province nor in the western U.S. of A. Unfortunately, Mitchell died in a light plane crash in the Farwell Canyon area the year after I conducted my interview with him.

After the interview, Mitchell asked us how far we hoped to get that first day.

"I had thought we'd make it to the Schuk's home ranch," I mused, "but given the hour this interview has ended, I know that would be too far to travel this evening."

"Well, then," Mitchell suggested, "why don't you drive the thirty odd miles to Riske Creek and another ten miles south to my cabin at Farwell Canyon? It has plenty of firewood and comfortable bunks."

"Sounds fine to me," I responded quickly, gratefully accepting his offer, and I was about to leave when he continued.

"Once you leave the highway south of Riske Creek, you should have no trouble finding the cabin. The road is good, but, " he added, "there is one wet spot."

Once outside his office building, however, Mitchell saw our vehicles, Poole's and my Jimmys, and remarked that with those we would have no difficulty getting through the wet spot.

It was a pleasant evening early in November—no moon, but plenty of starlight. Less than a couple of hours later, we were off the main highway and heading for the cabin. Sure enough, the wet spot was where Mitchell had said it would be: a wide pool of water about a hundred feet in length. In the lead vehicle, I drove ahead into the water, and…that's where I stayed for the next couple of hours!

I tried alternately gunning my vehicle forward, then reversing, but to no avail. I was stuck and so, right behind me, was Poole. There was no room either side of me for him to get by. Neither of our vehicles was equipped with a winch—something I made certain was corrected before my next upcountry trip, but since that was the first few months I'd had the Jimmy, I claim some excuse for my oversight. I did, however, carry a usually most useful item, a "come along" or cable puller. It did not prove that useful on this particular occasion. After a couple of hours of cursing and sweating and digging around the vehicle, Dan, who was behind the wheel while Poole and I sloshed around in the mud and water, called out that there seemed to be some movement to indicate perhaps we could get out of our predicament shortly. Sure enough, a few minutes more digging and laying branches fore and aft of the Jimmy and the vehicle under the Tigger's piloting exploded out of that hole, mud and water flying all over the lot, including Poole and me, as it roared up and out onto drier ground.

Before Poole tried taking his vehicle through, however, we double-checked the situation and discovered my left front wheel and left rear wheel had come up against two small boulders directly in line with each other a few inches below the surface of the water. It was one of those things that would never likely happen again in decades. As I initially tried to get the vehicle out, the more I gunned the motor, the deeper I jammed the left side wheels against those rocks and into the hole. Only after our digging and branch-laying efforts was Dan able to turn the wheels enough to get out. Poole sailed through without problem, and we arrived at Mitchell's cabin about midnight. A fortunate thing too, since it was after all November, and snow could have made things much more difficult had the gods not been smiling on us that otherwise clear and pleasant evening.

* * *

Then there is, or was, what came to be known over a number of years as the Tigger's rock. It was a couple of years after the Farwell Canyon incident. Dan was twelve or thirteen, and he and the fellow we'd dubbed the previous year as Smokey were with us.

At the time, we were camped on the shore of a sheltered and pleasant lake, Murray Taylor, named after a man who had ranched up there until his death a few years earlier. We had the four quarters of a moose wrapped in cheesecloth and hanging in the trees at our campsite. The bull had been shot a few days earlier and was in prime condition, particularly due to below freezing temperatures during the intervening nights. It was our second day at the lake. I had driven into even higher country early in the day, and we'd walked two or three miles back into the timber after what passed for a road had petered out.

On the way back to camp late that afternoon, as we approached an abandoned shack and behind it a no longer used airstrip, we saw a group of about twenty horsemen and women. They were dismounted, giving the horses a breather and taking pictures of the coast mountains to the west. I realised I'd never seen a more incongruous group of riders in my life. All of 'em—with the exception of a very attractive young blond lass, who we later learned was the guide for the group—were dressed in the most outlandish cowboy gear I'd ever seen. Chaps and Stetsons straight out of the western movies of the late twenties and early thirties that produced such screen heroes of that era as Hoot Gibson, Tom Mix, Buck Jones and Ken Maynard among others.

Turns out they were German tourists on a trail ride from the Chilko Lake ranch resort. Together with their heavily accented English and, to say the least, highly intriguing dress, I confess there is nothing more ludicrous than a passel of "Cherman" cowboys. Particularly when one comes upon a flock of 'em in a part of that high country where one rarely sees even a legitimate cowboy.

As we drove slowly by the mid-European visitors, they courteously waved us on our way, and we figured we'd seen the last of 'em. It was not to be. A couple of hours later they set up camp on the lakeshore half a mile from us.

Soon after Smokey and I had downed our evening quota of martinis (the Tigger, being then too young to drink anything other than fruit juice and ginger beer) and dinner was over, the boy started a fire. Moments later, a couple of the Germans walked in wanting to know if we had any cigarettes we could sell them. Doug Johnson (Smokey) had an extra carton, which he graciously proffered the visitors, gratis. After polite protestations on both sides, they returned to their camp, but not before inviting us over to join them for a glass or two of conviviality. This we did, which in some respects was a cardinal error.

Doug fell madly in love with the earlier mentioned blond leader of the German expedition. I must admit she was a damned good-looking gal, daughter of a transplanted American who had guided in Chilcotin country for many years, although by that time he spent his summers down in the U.S. and his daughter with him. The evening we were enjoying the Germans' hospitality, Smokey, in a fog of extreme conviviality and being hopelessly smitten, made her a present of the rack from the bull moose we'd earlier shot. Technically, I suppose, he was within his rights since, although he hadn't shot the animal, it was on his game tag and was in effect his first moose. The target of his romantic euphoria that evening had of course seen more than her fair share of moose as well as deer, elk and caribou racks, so she in turn presented one of the Germans with it, which didn't seem to bother Smokey. Whether the ultimate recipient of the rack was ever able to get it back to his native heath, we never found out. I do know that Doug, due to circumstances beyond his and her control at the time, was not able to consummate his brief but torrid love for the visitors' comely guide, and so far as I know he never heard from nor saw her again.

Prior to our going over to the visitors' camp that evening, the Tigger took off with his newly acquired 410 shotgun to search for grouse. He returned without any birds shortly before we went to spend time with the German crowd, and he told me he had spotted a buck mule deer. He'd followed the animal for a distance but wisely turned back as dusk began. In following the deer, however, he had to cross a road and at that point had placed a round rock about the size of a baseball on top of another rock, which was about four feet in diameter.

The next day we followed the buck's tracks some distance into the timber beyond where the lad had placed the rock. We never did see the deer. But for at least ten years thereafter, every time we drove along that road, we spotted there on top of the larger rock what became known as the Tigger's rock. Winter snows, summer rains, fall and winter winds hadn't shifted it. I always meant to stop and take a picture but never did. Sure enough, one later year when I decided I would stop and do just that, both rocks had gone. Most likely they'd been shoved aside by a grader when the road was subsequently widened.

A few years later, I met the fellow who was largely responsible for the German visitors being up there on that occasion. Since then, more and more German visitors have discovered the Chilcotin due mainly to the spadework done in that regard by Hans Dankel. He and wife, Karin, came out to BC a year or so prior to our meeting that group of incongruously dressed dude riders. Karin and Hans started a successful tourist business in 100 Mile House. Undoubtedly his regular return visits to Germany brought and continue to bring to that area of this province a steadily growing number of mid and west European tourists. In turn, the magnificence of Cariboo and Chilcotin country has become well known in Europe, particularly in Germany.

Dankel also in more recent years started what has come to be known as the Great Cariboo Trail Rides. Each summer he leads groups of tourists, Canadian and American as well as European, on riding and camping trips into the west Chilcotin. Not only has he become adept at outfitting and leading such jaunts, but he also wears a more modern style of western clothing than those visitors we saw those years ago.

During BC's 1986 Expo, it was Dankel who organized, outfitted and led a special tour from 100 Mile House through backcountry, following much of the old Gold Rush Trail of last century, all the way to Vancouver and the 1986 Expo. After taking part in the opening of the exposition, Dankel and his amateur roughriders took the same route back. I must confess I know of no other fairly recent newcomer to this province becoming as much a cowboy as has Hans Dankel, nor for that matter as enthusiastic a "Cari-booster." Among other things, Dankel is acquainted with Roland Jung, a German novelist who, since he visited Cariboo country to take one of Dankel's trail rides, has written extensively about that part of British Columbia.

In my pre-war visits to Germany as part of my early days as a fledgling journalist, I came to realise that many in that country were excellent horsemen. The German army teams, in fact, ranked high in the standings at the 1936 Olympics in Berlin. During my sojourn as a prisoner of war in that country, I saw many accomplished civilian and military horsemen. But never in my wildest imaginings, particularly those years as an unwilling guest of the Third Reich, did I ever think I'd one day see a "Cherman" cowboy, dude or otherwise, until I met and came to know Hans Dankel, a postwar trail-ride boss from the Cariboo!

Camper "bogged down" en route to Far Meadow
(Note tree halting roll over.)

CHAPTER 5
STOVEPIPE

It was by now late afternoon as I sat letting my idle mind wander back over the years and incidents already put before you. It was quiet again in the meadow.

I started to make my way slowly and quietly back to camp. It was still fairly warm, although a chill was beginning to make itself felt. That is the time of day in the wilderness I've always considered a sort of calm before the killing storm. It is one of those strange aspects of nature in the wilderness, shortly before dusk when predators are preparing for their night's hunt. There comes a period of stillness during which there is hardly any movement of trees or grass. A time of no wind. Neither bird nor beast is heard. It is tantamount to a deathly stillness. And perhaps that is what it is. A last hour of peace for the prey animals before they fall to claw and talon of their predators.

By the time I got back to camp at Far Meadow, it was full dark. Not unexpectedly, there was no sign of my son, although I had kind of hoped he'd be up with me that evening. But he would undoubtedly make it up there the following day.

As I walked into the campsite, I was put in mind of an incident three or four years earlier at the same place. On that occasion there were four of us: Dan, a longtime friend, Roy Slack, and his son Trevor. It was Trevor's first trip, he having only that year passed his CORE course and obtained his first hunting license.

We'd been hunting in a desultory fashion for a few days. Which means we really hadn't been working at it, although we had enjoyed, a couple of evenings earlier, a tasty and filling grouse and rabbit stew, the Tigger having shot both. Point of fact: that stew was talked about long after that particular trip, primarily because the evening I made it, doubtless emboldened by an extra ration of martinis, I threw in all manner of spices as well as healthy portions of potatoes, carrots, parsnip (and if I recall correctly, even a couple of eggs!). I can never remember precisely what spices and other ingredients beyond the staples I put into my evening meals, much less the amounts. However, none have yet complained and all seem to function quite well thereafter in all particulars.

Anyway, I had decided to move up country to the Far Meadow area, which I hadn't seen for a few years. It is good country and has in the past yielded moose, deer and plenty of birds. We'd left our previous campsite mid-morning and, about noon, halted for lunch on the near side of a ford across still another branch of Brittany Creek. After lunch, the two younger members of the party scouted ahead while Slack and I stretched out in the sun to doze.

We were jolted awake by the lads. "Dad!" each shouted simultaneously into the sleeping faces of the appropriate father. "The road's flooded!"

Sure enough, we were soon to discover that the far side of the ford was a couple of feet under water. The road we'd normally use to get across that stretch and up a pretty steep incline beyond there was also inundated. More to the point, it was very soft and soggy . Neither Slack nor I had any desire to get stuck in that mess. Both of us were for turning back. There was no way I could see that we'd get beyond that point without an awful lot of tree cutting. Even at that, it was well nigh impossible to cross the creek for a number of miles either side of the ford. The problem was caused by beaver that had dammed the area for a couple of miles down from us.

"Please, Dad," Dan and Trevor echoed each other again, "let us have a crack at finding a spot. Once we get the vehicles across the ford, we could cut our way up the hill on the far side, parallelling the road."

"It would take hours to do what you wish," I argued sensibly, but they kept up the pressure, and finally I gave in.

"We'll give it a try. But if it doesn't prove the strong possibility of getting through or around the morass before dark, we will all just forget it. Deal?"

"Deal!"

In less than two hours, they'd made their point and the beginning of their road around the problem area. My vehicle and trailer went through without problem. There was a tight moment, however, when Slack was taking the camper through. The vehicle slipped into a deep, soft spot. Had it not been for the fact the lads had cut around one tree instead of dropping it, the camper may very well have rolled. That tree saved us a wrecked camper and painful headaches!

Once we'd maneuvered through and around the dammed section, we began making steady progress until, as darkness fell, I lost the road—something which is not difficult to do, particularly after dark, more so when the road is little more than a trail. One other aspect to this is I have long had the habit to driving in backcountry after dark without using headlights but merely parking lights in order to aid or at least not greatly to diminish my night vision.

Fortunately, it didn't take long to find the trail again. Within half an hour we were out of the timber and at the edge of Far Meadow itself. The cabin and my usual campsite up there sits on a rise overlooking the small lake at the eastern end of the meadow. A lake fed by—would you believe?—Brittany Creek. At that point I finally switched on my headlights because the half mile or so to the campsite is covered with large clumps of wild grass. One has to know the area fairly well; otherwise the vehicle can get hung up—not the sort of thing a man wishes at the end of the day as he looks forward to getting set up for the night, having dinner and of course a taste of olive soup!

As I pulled in alongside the cabin, something moved in the headlights, and a cold feeling came over me. I stopped the vehicle. Slack, behind me with the camper, did the same. He doused his headlights, but I kept mine on and continued to watch. I couldn't make out what was moving around in the tall grass. For a brief spell, it went behind a storage shed and out of the lights. I still wasn't too keen on getting out of the vehicle because I thought it may be a wolverine, and that's one animal I have no urgent desire to tangle with. The Tigger is made of sterner stuff. He took my rifle and stepped down from the Jimmy, just as the apparition appeared around a corner of the shed.

Even the young fellow was taken aback somewhat. It was the strangest looking creature I've seen before, or since, in the backwoods. It looked something like a wolf but with the longest head and snout, all of two feet. For a moment, it reminded me somewhat of an anteater, an animal certainly not native to this province. It was running aimlessly back and forth, undoubtedly attracted by the light and the sound of our voices.

I was still not anxious to get out of the vehicle and examine it further. Nor did Slack move out of his vehicle. His son, however, jumped out to join Dan, and both ran forward and grabbed the animal. It didn't attack. Indeed, it seemed to become calm at the sound of their voices. It was an unusual scene. In the middle of nowhere, so to speak; under a night sky filled with stars, a sliver of moon just beginning to show above the trees surrounding the small lake in front of the deserted cabin, and the strange animal, now still, as the lads held it.

Slack and I finally left the safety of our vehicles. The Tigger came back to the Jimmy to dig out a pair of tin snips. The mystery was solved, and with it, a noticeable easing of my anal orifice. The creature was a young and very scared German shepherd. Its elongated "head" was in fact a length of stovepipe. The dog, lost or as is more often the case in the backcountry, abandoned, had doubtless gone after some small animal, possibly a packrat, which in turn probably ran into the chunk of pipe and out the other end. The dog got its head into one end of the pipe and couldn't free itself. Clearly it had been in that unfortunate and uncomfortable situation for some days, its ribs being easily seen under its hide.

In a matter of moments, Trevor and Dan had the piece of pipe off, and the dog, which they subsequently named Stovepipe, showed its appreciation by attaching itself to them for the next few days we stayed up there. That evening, while I prepared dinner and Slack and

I sipped an extra quota of martinis to calm our frayed nerves following our initial sighting of the strange creature of the Far Meadow high country, both lads fed and watered their new friend.

During the course of the remaining time up there, wherever we walked, Stovepipe, like Mary's little lamb, followed those youngsters wherever they went. While we hunted, the dog never barked but would circle around in the timber—which may have been the reason we saw neither hide, hair, nor for that matter feather of game those remaining days.

When we departed, not before the lads made sure a battered pan full of food was left for the dog, it was a much healthier and obviously happier animal. To the dismay of Trevor and Dan, but the unspoken relief of Slack and myself, Stovepipe seemed quite content to stay where we'd found him.

I hadn't gone back up there until this trip, but there was no sign of the dog on this occasion. However, on Christmas of the year that we found Stovepipe, Cliff Schuk sent the Tigger and I a book about Gertrude and John Roger, who came to this province from Saskatchewan in the fifties and who built the vast Chilco Ranch. Although I started hunting Chilcotin country about that time, I never met either. John was killed some years later while piloting his light plane up there, and Gertrude returned to her home province shortly thereafter.

In the flyleaf of the book, *Lady Rancher,* Cliff Schuk had written, "To Dan and Roy, the only 'ant-eater' hunters I've ever known."

"Stovepipe," after pipe removed

CHAPTER 6
TREED BY A WILD BOAR

To my knowledge there are no wild boars in Chilcotin country, nor for that matter anywhere else in this most magnificent of all provinces. Nor for that matter are there anteaters in British Columbia.

In my retrospective mood, however, the evening I was back at the Far Meadow cabin sipping my first martini as I got my dinner ready, the remembrance of Stovepipe put me in mind of a time back at the prison camp to which I have made earlier references, Hohenfels in Bavaria. Carl MacDonald, a fellow prisoner there, was from Australia. The progeny of a Scottish-born father and an Austrian girl who, like his father, had immigrated to Australia after the First World War, Karl had been serving with an Aussie infantry unit when he was captured in Greece in 1941.

Carl managed to jump from the train carrying prisoners from Greece to Germany. A couple of New Zealanders were with him, and the trio was able to reach Yugoslavia, where they joined and stayed with a partisan group through the winter of '41/'42.

One of the New Zealanders was killed. The other and Carl were recaptured by the Germans during a partisan raid early in the spring of 1942. They were fortunate to have been taken by a German army unit. Had they fallen into SS or Gestapo hands, given that they had been with a partisan group, it's highly unlikely they'd have lived. Yugoslav guerrilla fighters, whether they were with the original partisans led by Michailovic or fought with the subsequently more successful Titoists, took very few prisoners themselves. This

51

resulted in equally short shrift being extended to partisans taken by SS units or falling into the hands of the Gestapo. Carl MacDonald's escape from possible torture and death by being recaptured by a German Wehrmacht unit took him ultimately to Hohenfels, where we met.

With the coming of spring 1943 the traditional pastime of many of us "Kriegies," short for *Kriegsgefangenen* or war prisoners, came once again to full flower. Escaping. Someone once claimed that, during that particular spring and summer, there were more allied war prisoners outside the barbed wire, including prisoners on working details in farms and factories, than there were inside. Whether that was true, I never discovered. But it is a fact that with the coming of warm weather many Kriegies did decide to try their luck.

MacDonald and I decided we'd give it a go that spring as well. Initially he was all for trying to make it back to Yugoslavia to re-establish contact with his partisan friends. Although the idea greatly intrigued me, I figured it was too much of a long shot and a dangerous one at that. First we'd have to reach the Danube a few miles to the south of Hohenfels where it flowed through the ancient Bavarian town of Regensburg. We'd then have to follow the river east into Austria before breaking away to the south and, hopefully, into Yugoslavia without running afoul of German troops en route. Even assuming we'd get as far as Yugoslavia, we'd then have to make our way past or through more German units before we could possibly make contact with any partisan group. Of all the areas then occupied by German forces, the two most dangerous to those occupying troops were Russia and Yugoslavia. While underground groups were operating in almost all German-occupied countries, none were more merciless and gave less—if any—quarter to their enemies than did Yugoslav and Russian partisans. Nor did they expect mercy from their occupiers if and when they fell into German hands. All in all, therefore, Carl's idea of trying to make it into Yugoslavia was to my way of thinking an extremely dicey proposition, assuming we could get that far in the first place.

After much discussion, I was able to persuade him we would be better off trying a less dangerous and complicated route. Particularly because of its relative proximity to our Hohenfels base, Switzerland would be the better way to go, despite the fact that this was also the most popular route with escaping prisoners.

Undoubtedly aware of the fact that spring brought fanciful thoughts of escape to our minds, the commandant of the Hohenfels camp came up with an interesting decree. He was a time-serving, regular German army officer and believed it was a prisoner's duty to try to escape. However, if the prisoner didn't get at least twenty miles, some thirty kilometres, in the first forty-eight hours, Commandant Plammer reasoned that the prisoner wasn't really trying but was just out for a pleasant ramble in the Bavarian countryside. Thus, the punishment was fourteen days in the "cooler," with rations of bread, water and ersatz coffee only. If, however, a man made greater distance in the first couple of days out, and it was his first attempt, the commandant considered this a serious escape attempt, and the punishment was only seven days inside with regular rations. That is, soup every third day in addition to the regular bread, water and coffee. Those so penalized were also allowed their smoking privileges.

Another somewhat unusual sidelight to all escape attempts by way of Switzerland came from Swiss authorities themselves. If you did make it into that neutral country, Swiss officialdom laid down the rule that you had to be more than six kilometres or four miles inside that country or be in some way known to Swiss police to have been in that country for forty-eight hours before you could be turned over to your own nation's embassy or consular officials.

One immediate result of that particular rule was the continual breaking of windows in commercial establishments in towns along Switzerland's border with Germany because the best way to be officially registered as being in Switzerland was to spend a few days in a Swiss lockup. And of course the speediest way to do that was to heave a rock through a window, preferably with a gendarme as witness. I've never found out who paid the bills for those window smashing sprees, the Swiss or governments of the escaped prisoners' homelands.

Given the foregoing background and the facts that Switzerland was the closest target, the weather that spring was exceedingly pleasant, and the chances of getting shot while trying to escape— once outside the camp—were much less likely by taking the Swiss route. That is where MacDonald and I decided we'd make for.

Having decided on our target, we then had to alert the camp escape committee. This was made up of fellow prisoners who, as long as they served on that committee, elected not to escape but instead stayed behind to advise and help with escape plans, supply maps, documents, food and specially tailored clothing made from blankets and mattress ticking. In some cases, even facsimiles of German uniforms were manufactured.

To the uninitiated, this may seem far-fetched in the extreme. It must be remembered, however, that the Hohenfels camp of some five-thousand prisoners from all walks of life and every corner of the British commonwealth included men of almost every profession and field of endeavour one could name. There were pickpockets and forgers, some of whom had done time for such crimes in their homelands in peacetime. There were mapping experts, photographers (who used cameras purchased from German guards using that earlier mentioned medium of exchange, cigarettes) and the linguists. Often they were, in peacetime, university or college professors who had taught languages.

The escape committee had to be advised of any escape plans not only as a courtesy, but more pertinent, to make sure unauthorized attempts did not foul up other, sanctioned plans that required detailed and sometimes complicated preparations. The committee didn't always approve one's plans. Nor did they try to block them either as long as they (the committee members) were aware of what was going on.

MacDonald and I elected to make most of our own arrangements although we requested and received map and compass and the committee's help in creating our means of initially getting out of the camp. That was accomplished by the simple expedient of the two of us joining a group of Polish and French workers billeted in the nearby village of Hohenfels, who were employed building an extension of the cooler just outside the camp proper. Possibly the German powers that be figured there was likely to be an exodus of the usual escapees that spring and they'd better be ready to accommodate them.

We stockpiled our own basic rations, primarily chocolate, raisins and other dried fruit (again Canadian Red Cross parcels proved invaluable). We planned to live off the land for other staples, fairly easy to obtain by stealing from farms and field stockpiles once we were outside.

From the camp theatrical stores we obtained old French army uniforms, intending to pose as French workers. The committee also supplied us with the necessary documents for that masquerade. Both of us had a smattering of French, enough we figured to fool any Germans we might encounter, civilian or military. MacDonald, of course, due to his mother's influence during his boyhood, was fluent in German.

Came the day. A warm one in May. Following roll call that morning MacDonald and I, attired in our nondescript bits and pieces of French uniform, mingled with a crowd of fellow prisoners who, at the behest of the escape committee, gathered around the main entrance to the camp. Whenever foreign workers such as Polish and French were employed in and around Allied POW camps, the Germans had camp kitchen staffs provide coffee for them, or water with which to brew their own beverages. This of course allowed for socializing and trading between our fellows and the foreign workers. The guards rarely interfered in these social exchanges and often used them as cover for their own trading ventures.

It was easy for the two of us to join the workers as they subsequently were marched off to their cooler construction project. For the rest of the day, we wandered around with the others, piling and unpiling lumber and the like. With the help of the Poles and French, we were able to unobtrusively arrange lumber into a small but comfortable shelter in the centre of the pile. Shortly before the day's work ended, we slipped into the shelter and remained there until darkness. Small packs containing our field rations were already in the shelter, placed there by a couple of our foreign worker friends.

An aside to all this came when one of my fellow prisoners, a Scot named Art McGill, who had been a British Army permanent force member of the Cameron Highlanders, told me some time later he figured something was "on" that day. When he saw "Jax" on an outside working party, he said to himself, "Knowing what a lazy son-of-a-bitch you are, I knew you couldn't be out there to do any serious work!"

At day's end, MacDonald and I were settled in our cubby hole as the others marched away. We waited until well after nightfall before gently and quietly removing some of the lumber and heading off into the countryside. It was a moonless night, but there were plenty of stars to provide enough light for us to make our way steadily south and also allow us to skirt the village of Hohenfels about eight miles away. We reached a point a farther three or four miles beyond the village by the time of false dawn, found a comfortable spot in the forest and settled down for the day.

We were fortunate in that nothing and no one discovered nor disturbed us that day. That night we marched some twenty miles, using back roads and forest trails, putting us to the west and slightly south of Regensburg, where we holed up the second night. We reckoned we were something less than two hundred miles from the Swiss border. We hoped to get across at a point east of Basel. Our rations as of the end of our second day out were more than adequate. We were not eating as much as we'd originally thought. That is something I've noticed in later years when on hunting trips. I don't eat much nor do I feel that hungry when walking miles in the timber. Back then, it may well have been that both of us were in pretty good physical shape. That plus the excitement of being outside the wire and our optimism probably helped reduce our need for food. Though water was plentiful, we didn't drink nor seem to want to drink that much either. Decades later, during my early Chilcotin jaunts, I was told by Eric Collier, trapper, guide and author of the best seller, *Three Against the Wilderness*, that a person in reasonably good physical condition can go without food altogether for upwards of a week and without water for at least forty-eight hours and not suffer any ill effects. Collier also pointed out that there are very few areas throughout this province where one cannot walk in one direction for a day or two without finding water. He maintained that one of the problems with people who get lost in the bush was to panic and go into circles instead of either staying put and lighting a fire or, if they feel the need to move, marching in one direction until they strike water or a road.

We didn't think we'd have any problems on our trek that late spring of '43. Travelling on average twenty or so miles each night, assuming the weather held and our spirits and constitutions held up, we reasoned we could be at the border in ten or certainly a dozen more days or, more accurately, nights. For four more nights we travelled through well-manicured, forested countryside. Occasionally we took to roads through the woods, breaking away to skirt villages, and still encountered no problems. It is interesting to realise at this juncture of my narrative, in view of the fuss raised in recent years in this province by those unalterably opposed to much of present-day logging practices, that the protestors often refer to how well managed are European forests. By accident or design, they conveniently forget, however, that foresters over there have been clearing and replanting for decades—if not, in some instances, for centuries. Our forest lands, on the other hand, are still largely in their original wild state. I will admit some areas of British Columbia, where clear-cutting has taken place, do look messy when compared to most European and Scandinavian forests. Yet in the majority of cases our logging practices, once again not forgetting the few years they have been going on when compared to those older, longer established practices, are by and large pursued remarkably well. Finally, I personally do not believe I want to see our forests as well-manicured as those in Europe and Scandinavia. There is a certain magnificence to wild forest land and, for that matter, wild rivers, which no amount of manmade control can begin to emulate.

We had been on the march for a week without problem. The

weather remained comfortably balmy and we were now much closer to our goal than from our point of departure. We had managed to bypass a number of large population centres, including Regensburg and Ingolstadt, as well as numerous villages without detection. Anyone who escaped or made the attempt will know precisely what I mean when I say that, even though a man may be clad pretty well as much as other people and for all intents and purposes is a legitimate member of the local populace, a POW on the run nevertheless gets the distinct impression everyone is looking at him and everyone knows what he is.

Meantime we continued moving at night and with every mile we marched closer to the Swiss border, our spirits soared. We passed through magnificent country crowned with the ruins of old castles and wild ravines. From Regensburg we managed to stay to the west of the Danube and were now in the Black Forest area when disaster befell us.

Perhaps emboldened by our success thus far, we started walking one evening earlier than had been our normal practise. Dusk was beginning and we had already walked three or four miles when we heard a gunshot. It was not hard by us, but we both hit the dirt and crawled quickly and quietly into nearby brush. As we waited there, we couldn't see anyone. No one shouted. Indeed we didn't hear any voices. Nor were there any more shots. At the time I didn't give it much thought, but shortly thereafter I concluded it was indeed strange that someone had fired without first challenging us.

Minutes passed, and we decided cautiously to stand up and check the lie of the land. As we stood, a crashing in the timber off to our right brought us both sharply alert. I was closest to the sound and was wondering what in blazes was happening when a ferocious-looking beast charged out of the underbrush, heading straight for us. As suddenly as it had started its charge, it stopped and stared at us. Quickly deciding this was no place for us, we both turned and ran for it. The animal resumed its headlong rush. We knew we had no chance of outrunning it, so we scrambled up separate trees, just in time to avoid the curled tusks of a large wild boar. The onset of dusk had made it difficult for either of us to see clearly what it was when it first roared out of the undergrowth. Now there was no doubt. Nor was there any doubt it was angry, squealing and grunting and tearing at the ground just a few feet below our tree perches.

It wasn't long before the racket it made drew attention from elsewhere and another source. Out of the forest at almost the same place we'd earlier been crouched came a couple of fellows wearing Tyrolean dress: embroidered jackets; leather shorts or "lederhosen" and hats with the traditional shaving-brush-type adornment. Both were carrying lethal-looking guns. As they trotted into the clearing, the boar charged off into the trees, and for a heartbeat or two we thought we had escaped detection by the hunters. Not so. Two incidents brought our hopes to a sad end.

The first was when MacDonald, trying to gently climb higher, snagged his jacket. In trying to free himself, he slipped and accompanied this mishap with a typical Aussie curse, "My flaming…" oath. This naturally caught the attention of the gentlemen below, one of whom remarked in faultless English, "You fellows are quite a distance from camp." The camp he referred to was that which Paul Brickhill wrote of in his book, subsequently made into a classic movie, *The Great Escape.*

Realising we were in trouble, I made the second error when I tried to make some answering remark in my atrocious French. The same German repeated his earlier remark in equally smooth French. We were effectively trapped.

It transpired that both our captors were German frontline officers on leave from duty in France. They were out hunting with some brother officers and had become separated from the main hunting party while following the boar that had routed us.

Initially the Germans thought we were officers from the earlier mentioned camp. We didn't enlighten them, but when a check was made with that camp, no one answering either of our descriptions was reported missing. A more thorough check confirmed that situation, and we finally admitted which camp we were from. This brought expressions of admiration from our captors, given the distance we had managed to travel before they nailed us.

The first night of our recapture, we were fed in the servant quarters of the small castle where the hunting party was staying. We spent that night in a locked and barred room in the cellar. Next day, after our true camp origin had been established, we were marched under armed escort to a nearby village and there housed for a couple more days with a group of foreign workers, prepared to being returned to Hohenfels, and of course seven days in the cooler with regular rations since we had made much greater distance and been out longer than the parameters decreed by the commandant. An ironic sidelight to our being housed with the foreign workers prior to our return to Hohenfels was the fact that they were Yugoslavs. They were not partisans, but military prisoners who had been serving with King Peter's troops when taken by the Germans.

Thus was the first serious escape attempt foiled by a fearsome beast, an angry wild boar. Much more fearsome than seeing in one's vehicle headlights a half wild animal with a chunk of stovepipe on its head in the British Columbia backwoods some forty years later.

*Memorial at foot of cliffs climbed
by few "Royals" with Jax @ Dieppe*

CHAPTER 7
BULLS AND BEARS

Throughout all the years I have been fortunate enough to hunt and fish in this province, primarily as you've gathered in Chilcotin country but also on occasion the Merritt-Kamloops area, the Peace River—rightly called the country of the Big Sky—and the country south of Burns Lake, I've often posed this question to guides, ranchers, trappers, conservation officers and policemen as well as other hunters: what is the most dangerous animal in the timber? Apart from man, that is.

The grizzly has most often been given the title. But one evening in a cabin on the shore of St. Thomas Lake in Cyril Shelford's Omineca country, I heard perhaps the best and most detailed answer to my question.

I was on a fishing trip organized by the same Cyril Shelford, that one-time maverick MLA, something of a thorn in the side of his then leader and premier, W.A.C. Bennett, as well as being the *bete noir* of multi-national oil conglomerates during his years as a member of BC government. In the party as well were half a dozen men from Shelford's neck of the woods whose combined guiding and hunting experience amounted to some three hundred years. They included a boyhood friend of Cyril's, Alan Blackwell, many times president of the BC Guides and Outfitters' Association; and Jim van Tyne, a burly fellow of infinite jest who was, as his name indicates, of Dutch descent.

We were sitting around a fire outside one of van Tyne's cabins at his fishing and hunting base camp when I put my question. It triggered a raft of stories from each of 'em. The upshot of that evening's BS session, however, was a kind of saw off. Half of those fellows contended the grizzly is the most dangerous animal in the wild. The others just as determinedly maintained the most dangerous and unpredictable to be a bull moose in the rutting season and/or a cow moose with calf.

In all my years of wandering the backwoods, I've never actually seen a grizzly. I've heard 'em and have also seen their tracks, droppings and claw marks on trees. I have also witnessed a bull moose at full charge, and I was once treed for almost an hour by a band of wild horses. That happened only a few miles from where I was sitting that fall day in my retrospective mood. About halfway round a ten-mile circuit I was walking, I stepped around a clump of willow while following a game trail. Suddenly I faced a handful of mares and colts and an obviously possessive stallion. The mares and colts were skittish as I circled around them, but the stallion was clearly on the prod. His ears back, he started squealing and rearing, hooves slashing the air. He kept charging a few paces forward then stopping, so I decided discretion was better than valour. I climbed a large spruce even as he charged right across the clearing.

During the time the stallion had me treed, he continued alternately to charge, then back up, all the while raising and shaking his head and squealing. Finally, honour and status satisfied, he turned and led his small herd off into the timber.

I took my time before climbing down. Later back at camp, I related the experience to my partners, who claimed I could have shot the stallion or at least fired shots into the air. For my part, I had no wish to shoot a horse, period. As for firing a few shots, I'm still not sure that would have halted or turned the stallion, nor indeed the mares with colts, before I had a chance to get a safe distance into the tree.

Another occasion in Peace River country above Dawson Creek a couple of miles off the Alaska Highway, I witnessed the decidedly awe-inspiring charge of a bull moose. Three of us were walking quietly down a gravel road early one evening. It lacked at least an hour until dusk. My partners were a few yards ahead of me, moving along ditches on either side of the road. I was walking on the road but close to the right side, ready to move into the ditch should we spot an animal. The road curved to the right, willow and other brush giving plenty of cover if needed.

On the left and ahead was a stand of lodgepole pine. They were pretty thin trees growing fairly close together. In such country, Nature in her infinite wisdom has planned it so that the blades of the moose's rack or antlers rise more or less vertically from the head. This allows the animal to move easily and quietly through thickly growing timber. In other areas where there's more space between trees, the rack tends to grow out to the sides of the head.

As my partners ahead of me rounded the bend in the road, one of them signalled that he'd seen something. We all went to ground and crouching moved along the ditches. As I rounded the road bend and was able to look down the road where it sloped toward another bend about a mile away, I saw the bull moose the other partner had first spotted. The animal was a good half-mile away, browsing undisturbed in willow on the left between the road proper and the earlier mentioned stand of lodgepole pine.

We moved quietly forward as the bull, in turn, continued browsing and making leisurely progress in our direction. We reached a point where the distance between him and us was about three hundred yards. The partner to my right and a few yards ahead could contain himself no longer. He jumped out of the ditch onto the road and fired from a standing position. And missed. The bull raised his head at the sound but didn't move off. Instead, he stared in our direction. The eyesight of a moose is not particularly good, but its hearing is extremely acute, as is its sense of smell.

The now very excited partner levered another shell into the chamber and fired again. That second shot didn't hit the body of the animal but struck one of the palmated blades of his rack, which jerked his head up and around. He started moving…straight for us. As he got into full stride and charge, I dropped to one knee and was prepared to shoot when my excitable partner's head appeared squarely in my rifle sight.

"Get the hell off the road!" I yelled, but to no avail.

Now the bull was coming up the road like a locomotive with a full head of steam. I tried to get into position to fire without endangering my partner. He didn't fire again; instead, he stood in the middle of the road and, I suspect, was momentarily paralysed by the sight of a couple of thousand pounds of moose on the hoof heading right for him.

Suddenly a shot rang out from the left ditch. In my excitement, I had forgotten about the other partner, who was on that side. His shot hit home. The bull stumbled and went down on his fore knees. A second later, be damned if he didn't get up and renew his charge. The fellow on the right threw himself back into the ditch as the bull reached a point only a few feet from where he'd been standing. I fired, and from his position in the ditch he fired almost at the same moment. Both shots hit home. The bull went down again, but even as we moved forward to fire a finishing shot, that moose continued trying to get back on his feet. Borrowing from the lexicon of Spanish matadors, one could say of him, a truly brave bull.

Later, as we began gutting, skinning and quartering the animal, we realised why he had charged. Still standing a few feet into the stand of timber from where the bull had first appeared were a cow and calf.

It was well after midnight before we finished butchering the bull. Quarters of the animal were by then encased in cheesecloth and lying on poles alongside the camper to chill out overnight. As we turned in for the night, we could hear the cow and calf moving restlessly not far off in the trees.

Next morning they were gone. As long as the calf had its mother with it, it would most likely survive the winter. As we left later that morning, I hoped the cow was already carrying in her belly the seed of another brave bull moose to replace the one that died the previous evening, defending her and her calf against three of the most dangerous animals anywhere...men.

I still have standing in a shed at home the rack of that bull. The left blade has a hole about two inches in diameter—a reminder of the only occasion in my years of hunting in this province when I saw a bull moose at full charge.

A bull moose at the charge is one thing—a political moose something else again. More than once in my broadcast verbal wanderings in years past I have referred to Will Rogers as having been the Cyril Shelford of the American scene. Of course Rogers was for many years front and centre on the world as well as American scene long before Shelford reached the age of consent. I've long admired Shelford, who never went to school but did graduate *cum laude* from what Lord Baden Powell aptly called "the 'Varsity of life." Cyril got what formal education he acquired by correspondence, not a unique situation when you consider that many born and bred backcountry British Columbians did much the same in their formative years.

Unlike Rogers, I don't believe Cyril Shelford stuck strictly to cowboying. He ranched and homesteaded, which included some cattle herding on horseback, but I reckon he was, if anything, closer to God via Nature through his years of fishing, hunting and guiding. I got to know him in the early days of his public life, shortly after he was first elected as the member for Omineca in W.A.C. Bennett's government. His dry wit and devastating sense of straight-faced humour became an integral part of the BC political scene, beginning with his maiden speech in the provincial parliament—a speech I had the honour of hearing the night he delivered it.

It was the first session of the legislature for the fledgling Bennett Socred administration. Shelford drew attention to the fact that, in those days, before the Socreds had been able to make any major changes to policies of the coalition government they'd just shattered, BC liquor was watered. The new member for Omineca illustrated the point beautifully when he told the House he had driven to Burns Lake a few weeks previous to lay in liquor supplies for New Year celebrations. Among other items of liquid conviviality, he bought a case of rum. "And," said Shelford, "when I got back home, Mr. Speaker, I had a case of rum popsicles!"

The point was well taken by the new attorney general, Bob

Bonner, and in no time the practise of watering BC liquor was ended once and for all.

One of Shelford's more memorable stories, I stole and used on the air and on camera more than once to illustrate a political point. He first told it to me when we were discussing an upcoming federal election.

It was the first time out for a fellow who went hunting in BC's north country. Those were the years before the province brought in its excellent CORE (Conservation and Outdoor Recreation) program, which, among other attributes, makes it mandatory for any potential hunter to pass tests in game recognition, gun handling, survival techniques, map and compass reading as well as respect for other's property rights before one can obtain a hunting license and, in more recent years, a hunter registration card.

On this occasion, the neophyte Nimrod became separated from his friends. Late in the day, after following fresh track, which proved to be in fact the track of a bull moose, he sighted the animal foraging in a meadow. He shot and killed the bull then opened and gutted it in almost textbook fashion. Only then did he realise he was in trouble. He was miles from camp. Had no idea where he was. He carried neither compass nor survival gear. Not even matches. Night was falling...fast.

He fired the traditional three shots at ten second intervals, signalling that he was in trouble. When there was no response, he fired another group of three shots. Again no response. He had only three left and didn't want to run out of ammunition, so he shouted himself hoarse. There was still no response.

With nightfall, the temperature dropped sharply. In desperation, he finally decided that his best bet would be to crawl into the carcass of the moose, believing he stood a fair chance of surviving the night in that fashion.

Despite the discomfort of his position, he did manage to sleep fitfully through much of the night. When he awakened at first light, he came to the stark realisation that he had forgotten one very elementary fact. When temperatures drop, things contract. This had happened to the moose carcass. The rib cage effectively imprisoned him.

He yelled for help. Still no response. His shouts were wasted on the wind. He hoped with the rise of sun the accompanying warmth would allow him to squeeze out to freedom. The temperature, however, stayed well below zero, on the understandable scale, throughout the day. He knew he wasn't likely to survive another night in that fashion when a thought struck him. He remembered that in the last federal election he'd voted Liberal. That memory did the trick. As he later related, "I felt so small I was able to easily crawl out through the arse end of the moose!!"

The denouement can be applied to any political party—which I have since done on more than one occasion with, I might add, varying degrees of success and…listener and viewer reaction!

Another Shelford story brought down on the heads of a one-time colleague and longtime fellow journalist friend, Dick Lillico, and myself the wrath of the then Speaker of the BC Parliament, Hon. Bill Murray. I had dined that evening with Cyril in the legislative dining room, in those days perhaps one of the finest restaurants anywhere in British Columbia. I had asked Shelford's advice as to what to do if and when one encountered a grizzly in the timber.

As I have already remarked, I have never had the experience although I have seen plenty of grizzly sign. There was one time when my two partners and I had a quartered moose on logs and the carcass of a deer hanging on high trees at our campsite. That morning the three of us took off, looking for a stroll through the woods, in different directions. One fellow struck out directly behind our campsite, intending to circle that side of the road and return late in the morning. My other partner and myself walked out to the road, where he set off south for about a mile and then cut into the timber on the other side of the road. I walked a mile or so north along the road and cut into the woods on the same side. Both arranged to meet me back at camp after traversing a sort of lazy "B" if you will.

I was back before the others. I'd stowed my .303 in the camper and was sitting and taking pot shots with a .22 at a can on a nearby stump. When the second partner got back a short time later and I told him I had not seen any fresh sign, he asked me to walk out to the road with him. There he showed me fresh grizzly tracks. They came out of the timber on the other side of the road directly opposite where we were camped. The tracks were over his, and a few hundreds yards down the road they turned off into the trees on the side of the road where we were camped.

I realized then that I had been sitting there with about seven or eight hundred pounds of freshly killed meat nearby and a .22 rifle as my only weapon immediately to hand. Fortunately, the grizzly didn't visit us before we moved out fairly quickly that same day.

Back with Shelford and his dinnertime advice on emergent grizzly procedure. He told of a guide taking three Americans on a grizzly hunt. By the time they reached his base cabin on the shore of a lake at the foot of a hill, it was dark. Before turning in the guide explained he'd get up before first light, would start the stove and the coffee, then go out to check for sign. On his return they'd breakfast and plan the day's hunt.

Soon after sunrise next morning, the Americans were huddled around the stove drinking their coffee when they heard a crashing in the timber on the hilltop above the cabin. Looking out, they saw the guide running hell bent down the hill and, a few yards behind, a large boar grizzly. As he made time and distance downhill, the guide yelled, "Open the goddamn door!"

One of the Americans swung open the cabin door, and as the guide reached the cabin he stepped smartly to one side. The impetus of the charging grizzly carried the animal straight into the cabin. The guide leaned in to close the door, then turned and said to the stunned Americans, "There's one. Now I'll go back and get two more!"

On returning to the press gallery in the legislative chamber that evening, I re-told the story to Lillico. Now it must be understood, Dick Lillico has the strangest laugh I've ever heard—something like a cross between a burro in heat and the cry of a hunting hyena. As I finished the story, he started laughing, literally uncontrollably.

The proceedings in the chamber below us halted. Visitors in the public galleries looked over to see what was afoot. I ducked down behind the railings of the press gallery. Moments later, we were summoned to the office of Mr. Speaker. In descending the steep steps from the gallery, I topped Lillico's performance by missing a step and after a noisy descent, winding up in a heap at the bottom. Murray's subsequent lecture on House decorum and the role and status of those who are traditionally supposed to be neither seen nor heard, members of the so-called fourth estate, is something never to be forgotten by Lillico or myself. Nor shall I ever forget stories of political moose and cabin-bound charging grizzlies!

I mentioned earlier the matter of women in these backcountry areas. They have been known to handle grizzlies better than either politicians or hunters. For instance, Kate Schuk, known to hubby, Joe, and close friends as Katie but respectfully addressed to this day as mother by both husky sons, Cal and Cliff, is a born and bred Chilcotin lady. Quiet spoken and not known for verbosity, when she does speak, people listen and with good reason since she invariably makes cold commonsense. Cal and Cliff tell me she knows each and every beast ever to graze Schuk range by name and idiosyncrasies. She still rides herd on occasion, on family as well as cattle, I suspect.

There are still women of her calibre to be found in remote parts of this province, Cal's wife, Lynn, and Cliff's lass, Alyson, being classic cases in point. While theirs still could not be rightly described as a luxurious lifestyle, especially when compared with life in more populated centres, the younger Shucks are nevertheless more comfortable than were the early life and times of Kate and Joe.

Only within the last few years was power put through to the Schuk's home ranch. But a few miles away at Cal and Lynn's place and farther out where Alyson, Cliff and their brood live, generators are still the main sources of power. As I mentioned in an earlier chapter, upwards of thirty miles from the Schuk's Tatloyoko home ranch, luxury of a sort has come to the Timothy Meadow cabin in the form of a padded toilet seat in the outhouse. Light is now also supplied via propane-powered lamps. Those two luxuries were added by Cliff just prior to his marrying Alyson.

If Kate Schuk retains the ability and aplomb to ride herd where and when necessary on cattle and family, she also seems to have a natural bent for handling bears without any problem. For example, shortly before we passed through there on one hunting trip, Cal and Joe were working out back of the house when they heard a commotion among a flock of chickens pecking away in Kate's small vegetable patch. It was fenced off with chicken wire, which clearly didn't keep the birds from getting in anyway. At lunchtime, when Cal and Joe went to see what the fuss was about, they saw a large black bear in the vegetable patch. It was after the chickens. Neither of the men had carried a gun but both tried, without success, to shoo the bear out of there. As Kate came to the back door to announce lunch was ready, she quickly assessed the situation, went back into the house, returned with a rifle, dropped the bear with her first shot and went back inside to serve the meal. Not the sort of thing encountered by the average suburban wife and mum.

Another time Kate and Joe were camped at the foot of Potato Mountain a few miles from home. They were looking for stray cattle. They had also been having trouble from wolves and bears. Joe walked into camp at day's end in time to see a grizzly loping off up the mountain, and Kate, sans rifle or weapon of any kind, coming from that same direction. It seems moments earlier she'd heard someone or something moving through the bush toward camp. Thinking it was Joe, she called to him. When there was no answer, she walked a few feet into the trees, called again, and saw the bear about the same time it spotted her. As this story goes, she yelled, "Git," and the bear "got."

Cal later told me, "When Mother says, 'Git' no one argues, not even a grizzly."

Joe has often remarked to me, "If you see a grizzly, shoot the damned thing. They cost me money." During a more recent visit, he drove me out to one of his grazing areas to show me a new irrigation system he'd installed. Also he wanted to check on a Hereford cow with a calf. The cow had a large wound on her left front shoulder. While Joe hadn't seen the incident, he surmised a grizzly had tried to carry off the calf. The mother tangled with the bear, succeeding in driving it away even though it had slashed her shoulder. By the time we saw mother and calf, they were doing well, mother quietly grazing while her offspring, in the manner of calves, the calf jumped and ran around seemingly without concern.

Even though I have never yet come face-to-face with a grizzly, that's one animal for which I have a decidedly healthy respect. As I recall it was either Cyril Shelford, or perhaps Alan Blackwell, who once told me the only way to stop a charging grizzly is to hit the animal between the eyes with a handful of hot shit. And, my informant added, "If you're ever faced with one, don't worry. You'll have plenty of ammunition!"

To give another example of what is often unexpectedly required of wilderness or backcountry women, the story comes to mind of the wife of an RCMP officer at Alexis Creek. Until recently the living quarters of the NCO in charge of that detachment used to be above the detachment office and the cells. Later a separate house was built nearby for the OC and his family. Other members of the detachment live in trailers on a small hill behind detachment HQs. In one of those trailers one early summer morning, the wife of the officer was sweeping out their quarters. Their offspring were in school and hubby was out on patrol. The lady glanced up from her chores to see a grizzly about to climb up the steps to the trailer, the door of which was wide open. More annoyed at the intrusion than panicked, the lady chased the animal away with her broom before returning to her domestic duties.

As the sergeant later explained to me, had it been a mouse, all hell would have broken loose, and doubtless her screams would have been heard well beyond Alexis Creek. As it was, no one heard about the grizzly incident until she casually mentioned it to the family at dinner that evening.

Such stories are not unusual, I gather. Another is told of a lady who lived alone way back in the Chilcotin range. She reportedly killed a grizzly as it charged her right outside her cabin—dropped the animal with one .22 shell through one eye and into the brain.

My son has been closer, knowingly, to a grizzly than I. That occurred one time when we were after deer on the south side of the

Chilcotin River a few miles east of Henry's Crossing. We were camped at the top of a ridge, and Cliff Schuk rode in on what I believe is known to initiates as an Enduro, a motorcycle designed for rough-country riding. For some years prior to his marriage and even though we may not have checked in with his parents or brother Cal on our way through to the high country, Cliff would spot our trail and would often take a day or two off to track us down. Then, if he wasn't able to spend the night with us, he'd certainly stay for dinner and a glass or two of conviviality. It was Cal's lady, Lynn, of all the Schuk clan, who first became mildly addicted to my martinis. Thereafter Cal and Cliff were not averse to sampling them. Only fair really when it's remembered that those two introduced me to the Schuk Shake.

The time the Tigger came closest to a grizzly, he was with Cliff. The day Cliff motorcycled in on us, we were getting ready to walk down to the river from our camp to look for deer. Roy Slack and his lad Trevor were with us, but when Cliff showed up, Dan decided to go with Cliff while the Slacks would hunt with me. We agreed to meet late in the afternoon at the river.

We three reached the rendezvous before the others. We hadn't seen anything, and since we hadn't heard any shooting, we figured neither had Cliff and the Tigger. When they did appear and were asked the stock question, Cliff remarked, "Since I was the guide, so to speak, I'll let the hunter [Dan] tell you."

"Well," Dan began, barely suppressing his excitement, "shortly after you three went your separate way this morning, Cliff saw movement ahead of us in the bush. We both followed the animal at a steady jog for a while, and then I guess I sort of got eager and raced ahead of Cliff. I stopped to check some tracks, and when Cliff caught up with me he said that we were chasing, not a moose as I'd thought, but a young male grizzly!"

We perked up at that news, knowing Cliff is always accurate in reading animal tracks. "So how did you react to that, Tigger?" I asked. My son's succinct reaction was just what I would have expected: "Oh shit!"

"I figured the animal was looking for a place to den up for the winter," Cliff concluded with a smile at his "hunter" companion.

73

The first time I ever took Dan into the backcountry brought a grizzly story. It was his seventh birthday and I took him out of school to spend a couple of weeks with Alan Blackwell for a tour of his guiding area south of Burns Lake. When I told the boy's school principal of my intention, he said, "Go with my blessing. He'll undoubtedly learn more in those two weeks than in a month or more in a classroom." Now retired, Syd Parsons was one of a slowly declining breed of teacher. Possessed of the priceless knack of dealing fairly, realistically, albeit sternly when needed, he also had that rare ability, so vital in shaping young minds, to arouse their interest and curiosity and not numb their senses with dull routine and repetitive rote—a situation that, I fear, has become more the rule than the exception in that profession in the years since.

My arrangement with Blackwell was to meet in Prince George after he'd seen the members of his last guided hunt of the season to their plane and on their way home. He figured that would be early afternoon and we could then drive leisurely back to his place in time for supper. Dan and I reserved a day room at a PG hotel since our flight into that town would get in mid-morning. Not long after we were settled in to await Alan's arrival, his wife phoned to say he'd be delayed but would meet up with us early in the evening.

The cause of the delay was not an isolated case, particularly involving Americans. That last morning of their hunt, Alan took the eldest visitor and his nephew across Eutsuk Lake. He stationed the older fellow on the far shore with instructions to patrol back and forth for a mile or so, always within sight on the lake. Alan would take the nephew in the backcountry for a couple of hours.

When they returned, the uncle was nowhere to be seen, so Alan left the nephew there, making it clear in other than polite language that he'd better stay put. Blackwell then set off to find uncle. He made a circuit through the timber of sixteen miles before he found the man, unharmed, but totally lost. Needless to say, Alan was not in too convivial a mood as they packed up and left on the two-hundred-mile trip to Prince George. In any event, we didn't meet until about eight that evening, and since Alan was extremely tired, I drove back to his home base while he and my seven-year-old slept.

74

A few days later, while Dan and I were still with the Blackwells, my wife, known to the family as "she who must be obeyed" or when her mood is such and the occasion warrants, as Her Royal Highness, happened to read in one of the Vancouver dailies a story about an American shooting a grizzly that was subsequently recorded by Boone and Crocket as a record bear. The animal weighed some twelve hundred pounds, measured nine feet and a couple of inches from nose tip to tail and, when later dried out, the skull measured sixteen and a quarter inches across.

What caused my lass Lila's hair to stand on end was that the guide for that hunt was Alan Blackwell. The American who'd shot the grizzly was the fellow Blackwell spent most of that day we were to meet, hunting for on the other side of Eutsuk Lake.

It took me some time after Dan and I returned home to convince his mother he was in no danger during the two weeks we spent with Alan. Even so, HRH had some severe things to say about my ancestry and origin when we first got home!

The great bear, the grizzly, is truly the monarch of our wilderness. Indeed the two animals considered to be the most representative of the Canadian backwoods are the moose and the grizzly. Despite my never having met one, over the years I have come to regard *Ursus Arctos Horribilis* with awe and admiration. The first and second of those titles mean bear in Latin and Greek respectively. It shouldn't take much imagination, much less a knowledge of classics, to know what is meant by the third!

Fearsome; terrible; horrible when enraged; nevertheless the grizzly, without a shadow of doubt, is a truly magnificent animal. Out of a welter of stories of actual incidents as well as legends galore, reports of a rampaging grizzly seem to involve man's carelessness, foolhardiness, or both, rather than the bear's unprovoked aggressiveness. There are well-documented cases of grizzlies wrecking campsites, cabins and even vehicles; grizzlies injuring and killing people; slaughtering cattle and sheep. One such case told of a grizzly in one American state killing over a thousand cattle during a fifteen-year period, another of an animal that lived more than thirty years, at times killing cattle. Both were said to have died from natural causes and, although seen on numerous occasions by skilled hunters and guides, managed to elude them without much difficulty.

Unlike the wolf, with rare exception, the grizzly kills to eat, not merely for the hell of it. It has also been said he is an animal that not only walks but also reasons like a human and can outwit man far more often than the reverse. I can well believe it. Having walked hundreds of miles in the wildest of country over the years I've hunted and fished this province, I'm convinced the main reason I haven't yet come face-to-face with a grizzly is simply that they've avoided me and I was completely unaware of their proximity. I've often heard ranchers and other hunters and guides point out that the great bear much prefers to avoid confrontation; until and unless you startle the animal or, much more dangerous, come between a sow and her offspring.

The story of Kate Schuk shooing away the grizzly on Potato Mountain, the experience of the RCMP officer's wife at Alexis Creek, and Cliff Schuk and the Tigger unknowingly chasing the bear would indicate how the animal will do its best to avoid confrontation. At the same time, however, it should not be forgotten that the grizzly is the most powerful and individualistic of bears and, like all wild animals, is unpredictable.

Usually when and where attacks on humans occur, there is reason for such incidents. The late Bill Dennett, in earlier years one of Canada's outstanding, prizewinning news photographers when with the *Vancouver Sun* (and after that an incomparably good TV news cameraman with what is now BCTV) was also a lifelong hunter. Years before I fell under the spell of Chilcotin country, Dennett often flew into, hunted and fished up there. One time he and his two regular partners came face-to-face with an angry grizzly.

All were seasoned hunters. All were excellent marksmen. The way Dennett told it, all three tried to avoid a head-on collision and backed up along the trail. The bear charged anyway. According to Bill, the three of them put upwards of a dozen shots into that bear, all the while backing down the trail, and still he was coming at them.

Finally he went down. They later discovered the animal was suffering from a festering hind foot. Apparently someone had wounded the animal some time before, and it was clearly evident that the bear, rightly, had no love for humans.

At the other end of the scale is Tommy Tompkins' story of the life and times with grizzlies. A former Vancouver police officer, he quit the force following a great personal tragedy. Thereafter he took up, full time, wildlife photography and filming. Over a span of thirty years, often for months at a stretch, he lived with, photographed and shot thousands of feet of film of the great bears in their wilderness habitat. Once he spent three months with a family of four, the boar, sow and two cubs, often operating his camera no more than thirty yards from the animals, even when they were feeding. Not once during that episode nor in all the years he spent with grizzlies in the wild was Tommy Tompkins attacked.

I knew Tommy when he was on the Vancouver force. Numerous times during his later years as a wildlife photographer I interviewed him. It is perhaps emblematic of things Canadian that, though he came to be one of North America's most expert and knowledgeable wildlife cameramen, he was never accorded the recognition and laurels he so richly deserved from government, nor any institution for that matter, during his lifetime. The CBC, on very rare occasions used some of his excellent work but neither that taxpayer-rich organization nor such as the National Film Board, much less private television outlets, made full use of his extraordinary talents. Disney material seems far easier to obtain and is less costly, it would seem.

CHAPTER 8
TEE PEE

It was comfortably warm in the Far Meadow cabin. The stove was stoked. My well- aged Coleman lamp was hissing along uninterruptedly, and I didn't really relish the idea of making the trip out to the small building with the quarter moon cut into the door, even though it was only a few yards from the cabin. While it was a clear, star-bright night, it was below freezing out there; but one must respond when the devil drives and the bowels need to be relieved. So, TP (toilet paper) in hand, out I went to answer nature's call before turning in for the night.

Tee Pee is a most essential item on all backcountry trips. Variously dubbed, Tee Pee, the Prayer Roll, the Comfort Coil, Man's (even on occasion I suppose also Woman's) Best Friend is a must. It is one item of our supplies I always make sure is in plentiful supply.

When on our walks into the woods, I have introduced newcomers on our trips to the vital necessity of carrying a goodly supply, particularly after a healthy meal and more so after a mug or two of my camp coffee. There are those who have pointedly described my gunfire coffee, the first of the day, as an infallible eye-opener. Further, if the eyes are not fully open by the time one has ingested that first mugful, one's vision is guaranteed to be speedily cleared after a dash to a suitable place in the bush, there to find moments of blessed relief; a spell of talking to the trees in silent, often welcome prayer or generally just to commune with nature as one attends to this necessary natural function.

It is my long-held contention that one should be as comfortable as possible in the timber, even when on occasion one may have to sleep under a vehicle, in a tent or under the trees. I suppose there are seasoned old-time fishers and hunters, more so those who live year round in the backwoods, who may look somewhat askance at my contention, but I have never subscribed to the idea of "roughing it" just for the sake of roughing it. Which is why I've never agreed with the opinion of some pioneer residents of wild country that, "If there's one thing that brings a fellow back to basics, its wiping his ass with a handful of leaves, marsh grass or wet moss."

I admit one cannot read a comfort roll as country folk used to read Eaton's and Sear's catalogues before putting the pages to more immediate use in the relative privacy of the outhouse. But TP can be used in a variety of ways: gun cleaning, rod cleaning, glass polishing (the spectacle as well as olive-soup-type glass), even fire lighting when necessary.

It invariably happens on our return home from backcountry jaunts, that my lass will find pants or jackets that need her cleaning expertise and, sure enough, in at least one pocket will discover wads of TP. I've often used a handful of it stuffed in a pocket to prevent loose shells rattling around when one is wandering in the backcountry.

During my time behind the wire in Germany, we received from some group of undoubtedly very concerned and dedicated ladies of some religious organization, the name of which I can no longer recall, packets with the title "Spiritual Food Parcel." They were, in fact, neatly bound copies of psalms and the New Testament. I can honestly say that every one who ever received them read every psalm and segment of the New Testament in detail. Usually this was done half a dozen pages at a time in the one instance, or singly in another. The holy writ was printed on rice paper and made excellent toilet tissue and cigarette paper. I most sincerely hope the ladies who so lovingly wrapped and sent out the "Spiritual Food Parcels" never ever discovered to what use their most welcome gifts were ultimately put!

Even as that night at Far Meadow I had to go outside for my last sojourn of the day in the outhouse, I also recall this was not only a necessary duty each night in the camps but also gathering at the latrines was something of a day's end social event. People then and there were in the habit of exchanging news and views, trying to run down the latest rumours, update ideas on when and how the war would end and even to do some trading.

At Hohenfels, due to the size of the camp, the latrines consisted of two massive buildings, each containing forty holes per side, each hole separated by a wooden partition. No doors, of course. In the centre of both buildings were two troughs, which ran the full length of the structures. They were for relieving one's bladder, and it also made it easy for fellows sitting in the little "prayer cubicles" to chat with those standing at the troughs.

The latrines were emptied of their contents once a week by way of a local civilian contractor who drove in with a truck carrying a large, oval-shaped tank, something like an oil tank truck. It came to pass that a heavy Allied air raid included Regensburg as part of one night's target area. The damage was extensive, and so the "honey wagon" didn't visit our camp for two weeks or more. In the interim, the effluent and paper rose higher in the trenches below the latrines. One evening, as he sat to contemplate his lot before turning in, one fellow was nipped on his family jewels by a rat scurrying along the top of the odorous pile just below the toilet seats. The injured fellow had to be taken promptly to the camp hospital to make sure he hadn't contracted rabies or, perhaps more serious so far as he personally was concerned, his future social prospects were not irreparably damaged.

Every evening thereafter, whenever one made his last call, it became the practise to strike a match and peer down the hole to make sure no beady little eyes were reflected in the light of the flame. One such evening, as one of the cubicles became vacant, I sat down to await the expected. Moments later, the unexpected happened. The first seat on the row had just been occupied by a chap who had performed the match-striking routine. Even as he sat down, all of us to his left, all the way along the row of holes on that side (myself included), sprang up one after the other much in the manner of targets in a shooting gallery—each of us clasping our hind quarters and giving forth with shouts of mixed rage and pain. The paper on top of the piled effluent had caught fire and wafted all down the line.

Fortunately, the flames flickered out when they reached the other end of the building without doing any further structural harm. That night, however, a number of us, including myself, slept on our bellies to give some relief to our scorched derrieres!

A day later, the honey wagon returned to regular duty, for which we were all duly thankful.

Inside Timothy Meadow's cabin showing "legendary" coffee pot

CHAPTER 9
THE VIKING AND THE BULL

We called him the Viking because he was born in Norway. Nick Bergum spent his boyhood on his parents' farm in that country and went to sea in his teens. For the next couple of decades, he sailed the world learning, among other skills he learned those years before the mast, to become a ship's carpenter. He returned home, married Inger, and both immigrated to this country in the mid fifties. Neither spoke much English. Nick got jobs on construction projects as a labourer; Inger went to work as a domestic.

It is a measure of the guts and determination of the majority of immigrants to Canada in the immediate post-Second-War years that they came here, to paraphrase John Fitzgerald Kennedy, asking, "Not what their new country could do for them, but what they could do for their new country." They went looking for and invariably finding work—not welfare. They did not ask for nor demand taxpayer-supported subsidies to learn our language. They taught themselves, more often than not at their own expense.

Over their next twenty years in this province, Inger and Nick Bergum prospered and finally settled in a delightful seaside home, much of it renovated and reconstructed by Nick at Qualicum. They subsequently turned it into a successful and, as our family can attest, very comfortable summer resort known as Bergums' Beach House.

My wife discovered Bergums' in the seventies. For the next dozen years we spent summer vacations there, during which times we introduced the Viking and, as we dubbed Inger, the Snowqueen to the joys of day's end martinis and on occasion the magnificence of Mozart.

During our Qualicum visits, the Bergums saw many of the pictures I'd shot on my Chilcotin trips, and one day Nick asked if he could join me on my next safari. And that's how we found out that the Viking snored.

Now, throughout my years on this mortal coil I have been treated to, more accurately, perhaps, victimized by...snorers. At school there were fellows who could keep a dormitory awake half the night with their "snorking" rather than just plain snoring. In the army and during the time I spent behind German barbed wire, the nocturnal concertizing of some had been known to bring about near homicidal tendencies in those forced to suffer this torment.

I recall a couple of methods used, with limited success I will admit, to get back at our tormentors. One was to gently shake the snorer to semi-wakefulness then ask him if he'd like to buy a battleship. Another was to stand alongside the offender pouring one full tumbler of water into an empty glass, repeating the process for a few minutes, then slipping away to one's own bunk. Sure enough, it wasn't long before the snorer came groggily awake and would stumble outside to relieve his bladder. This ploy rarely put a permanent end to their snoring, but it did give a man a kind of gleeful albeit brief spell of deep satisfaction—more so if you could fall asleep before the racket started again.

I have to confess, however, despite the foregoing, that I have never, ever heard any human being snore as did the Viking. In the confines of a camper way back in the timber, it is little short of devastating. I did my damnedest, on that first Chilcotin trip for Nick, to feed him strong doses of Mozart and martinis, hoping to relax him enough to allow Roy Slack and myself to get to sleep before the old salt struck up his discordant concertizing. That ploy rarely succeeded. One night, however, things didn't go well from the start. It was Slack who got things off to a less than auspicious beginning.

All three of us were drifting off after a good dinner and a goodly ration of olive soup. The strains of a Mozart piano concerto issued softly from my cassette machine. The music was accompanied by the gentle sighing of a wind through a grove of aspen outside the camper.

Suddenly, from somewhere inside the camper came the tinny sound of "The Yellow Rose of Texas." It certainly wasn't part of my repertoire on cassette.

"What the (expletive deleted) is that?" Nick and I wondered out loud. Slack had the answer. One of his sons had loaned him a watch, which played that damned refrain at a previously specified wake-up hour, except the watch had been wrongly set. For almost an hour we looked for that timepiece; all the while the tinny tune kept playing. Ultimately Slack discovered the watch stuck in one of the corners of the overhead bunk. Once more peace was restored.

Soon after first light next day, I was rudely awakened by a God awful sound—something between a blunt saw ripping into green lumber, the belly rumbling growl of a sow grizzly in heat, the spitting snarl of a dyspeptic wolverine or a combination of all three with something added. It was the Viking, snoring at even greater intensity and decibel level than usual. I was out of my sleeping bag in seconds, cursing and blinding at him having had no effect. A couple of good thumps did the trick. It now being full daylight, I put on the coffee. As I was adding a couple of handfuls to those already in the pot (I never get rid of the grounds until the pot is half full), damned if Nick didn't start in again.

I turned around to ream him out, and there he was, wide awake. The shattering sounds continued from outside the camper!

I opened the door and looked down at a massive Hereford bull. His head was swinging from side to side, and he was bellowing and snorting in a decidedly aggressive fashion. When he caught sight of me he backed up, pawing the ground and throwing up clods of earth; he seemed to be getting ready to charge. I grabbed a rifle and fired a couple of shots into the air. The bull hesitated, backed up a few paces, made a half-hearted charge forward, then swung up his great head, let go another deep-chested bellow, and trotted off seventy or eighty yards to join his small harem of cows, honour and status clearly satisfied.

We concluded that the bull, hearing Nick's admittedly unusual and some may say inhuman snoring, probably believed the camper either was, or contained, a rival for his cows.

Providence was undoubtedly with us that morning. Otherwise I'm certain the bull would have charged right into the camper, and Lord knows what damage he may have inflicted on the vehicle, if not also us.

In retrospect, I've often thought of the traditional picture of a Viking, a barbaric-looking fellow wearing a conical-shaped leather helmet from which protruded steer horns, and I've wondered if maybe that Hereford bull was a reincarnated Scandinavian bull; or conversely, if Nick himself ain't a reincarnated Viking with a bit of fighting bull thrown in for good measure!

Perhaps strangest of all though, neither Slack nor I heard anything but the gentlest of snoring from our Viking partner the rest of that trip.

The next, and sad to say the last, time I took Nick Bergum up country, my son was along too. Slack was not. We were camped once again by Taylor Lake, the spot where some years before we had encountered the German "cowboys." Nick didn't get up to the Far Meadow country on his first trip, so I decided to take him there for one, possibly two, days. One morning after breakfast we took the Jimmy and trailer and headed off, leaving the Tigger with the camper and the boat so he could try fishing if he didn't want to go hunting on his own.

About an hour later I missed the trail at a point near the end of an unnamed lake. That lake is roughly a couple of miles long and no more than four hundred yards across at its widest section but beautifully situated for, at its far end, the coast mountains dominate the whole vista.

I got to know of the lake, and subsequently Far Meadow and the dozen or so miles between, by way of my first conversation with Henry Lulu, also known as Eagle Lake Henry. Indeed, Henry's Crossing a few miles back where a bridge crosses the Chilcotin River is said to be named after Henry, he having been, I gather, a Chilcotin band chief.

The first time I ventured along a side road on the south side of the crossing, I saw Henry's cabin situated in a magnificent setting. From the little verandah built along the front of his cabin he had a panoramic view of a small lake, in the middle of which was a tree-filled island and, beyond, a sweep of country miles wide in which could not be seen any other human habitation. Rising majestically in the west was a broad segment of the Coast Range—truly a multi-million-dollar view.

The old Indian was sitting on his verandah sunning himself as I drove up and got out to chat. When I asked if there were moose in the area or in the country back of his place where the road wandered off into the trees, he grunted and shook his head. "No moose here. Moose way west over far mountains," he offered, pointing to the range, which was all of forty or more miles away. I went back to the vehicle and returned with a bottle of gin and a box of shotgun shells, which I presented to him as I asked his permission to drive through his property.

He acknowledged my tribute with the ghost of a grin and remarked, "Plenty moose that away," gesturing along in the direction of the road behind him.

Some three or four miles along that road we came upon the earlier mentioned unnamed lake. It was late in the day, so we pulled off the trail and set up for the night. Before darkness descended I took a short walk down to the end of the lake, where I saw a number of game tracks. The very next morning, one of my partners shot a young bull moose at the far end of the lake, which necessitated packing quarters, heart, liver and rack two and a half miles over and through the trees and over some pretty thick windfalls as well as young timber growth. Mark you, that was years ago, when I was somewhat younger and more vigorous. In those early years too, the Tigger was still in his infancy and so wasn't along to help with the packing.

For a number of years thereafter, I always presented Eagle Lake Henry with what came to be a traditional gift of gin and shells, until one year I found the cabin empty. He had died that spring. One of the things I can never forget about that stout, stocky man was that every time we saw him, he was either about to ride off to hunt or had just returned. He once explained to me, "I do the hunting; my woman does the cleaning, skinning, plucking and cooking." There is much we white males can learn from our native Indian brethren!

We've taken a couple of animals from the area around that lake in intervening years, but not lately. Even so, I have always seen track somewhere in the vicinity.

The morning I briefly lost the trail when taking Nick Bergum through there, I happened to glance back to the lake. Standing in the shallows, feeding on lily pads, was a young bull. He hadn't seen us or, if so, he certainly wasn't disturbed. Nick was still sitting in the Jimmy chuckling over my losing the trail when I said, "Take a look at your first moose."

That remark, in retrospect, could be classed under the heading "famous last words." Before I could say or do anything further, Nick was out of the vehicle and firing. "Take it easy," I yelled to him since the distance was far too great from where we were for accurate shooting. He paid no attention. He had already shot off one magazine and was reloading, so I thought I'd better have a go just in case. All the while, the animal continued feeding. I knew my shots weren't bang on. It was a new rifle, the weapon I'd had for many years together with my other guns having been stolen during a break-in at our home earlier that year. I hadn't yet taken enough time to become familiar with the new rifle, although I targeted it in at a range, no longer there unfortunately, that used to be off the road just west of Alexis Creek.

Meantime, a couple of shots from Nick's second magazine and the moose jumped, then loped off across the end of the lake and into the tall timber. It didn't appear to be in trouble as it disappeared, but as I well know, an animal that size can and often does run for two- or three hundred yards before dropping, even though it may be hit in the chest cavity. About the only hit that will bring down a large game animal where it stands is a brain shot, a particularly difficult shot even for the best of marksmen.

I was finally able to calm Nick down and after waiting a few minutes, we set off to look for the animal or a blood sign. I walked into the trees a hundred yards or so above the lake on the side where the moose had bolted and told Nick to walk along the shore to the other end of the lake. There we'd meet, assuming I hadn't spotted the animal down, and we'd compare notes.

I soon found the tracks, but after more than an hour of scouting and scouring that side of the lake, I concluded the animal wasn't hit but was most definitely an "educated moose" and was likely still running. What puzzled me, however, was why it had jumped after that last shot of Nick's. We met as arranged at the far end of the lake, and when we reached this end, I walked across to where the moose had been feeding. It didn't take long to realise what had happened. Nick's shots had been dropping short and one had hit a rock below the animal's belly. A sliver of rock must have stung the bull and off he went.

On pacing off the distance from that point to the vehicle, it measured over five hundred yards. Our rifle sights were set for two hundred!

The last day of that trip we dropped in to pay our usual courtesy call on Kate and Joe Schuk, and while sipping Joe's favourite brand of conviviality, gin and orange juice, told the story of Nick's first moose. Joe thought for a moment, then in his slow, calm drawl, he opined, "Well you know, at five hundred yards, a person might have to use a scope." Both our rifles carried scopes. Joe's doesn't!!

In the very same spot at the end of the very same lake some years after, there were four of us—the Tigger, Slack, a fellow named Rick Upton and myself. As we approached the lake that afternoon, for the first time in the time I've travelled that particular area, we found we were not alone. A couple of Americans were camped there along with Eagle Lake's nephew as their guide. That morning they'd shot a bull at roughly the same place where Nick saw his moose. They had just finished butchering their animal and were about to move out. We camped a few yards down the trail and started setting up for the night. In less than an hour I was preparing dinner and mixing the evening's ration of martinis for Slack and myself (Upton and Dan being staunch drinkers of what I've long called aerated maidens' water, local beer!). I glanced down at the end of the lake and, sure enough, there stood another bull in the very same spot where Nick's first and only moose had stood. Particularly unusual on that occasion was the fact that the American party were still packing up after spending much of the day butchering their game, only a few yards from where the newcomer was standing and feeding. And there was activity and noise from our party too.

Slack and Upton leapt out of the camper in one bound, loaded their rifles and ran down toward the lake. Dan was right behind them, but as they started firing he refrained, for fear he might see one of them in his sights. Now the animal was moving in the same direction taken by the moose Nick had educated.

This time the bull was neither hit nor stung as it ran into the timber. We trailed it for a mile or more, but it was still moving steadily. As dusk was falling, we turned back to camp. Later that evening when the lies and liquid conviviality were flowing well, we heard wolves from the direction that the moose had taken. Whether they subsequently took the animal or were trailing something else, we never discovered.

One other incident near the same lake stands out. A few years before we'd encountered what came to be known as Nick's and Upton's moose, the teenaged son of one of my earlier partners came into possession of a series of taped moose calls. As usual, I had a cassette machine on the trip, and early one September evening he and I sat at the far end of the lake and played calls for an hour or so. Nothing happened.

The following morning when we tried the calls again, there came an answering call some way ahead of us in the trees. We headed in that direction and shortly came upon new tracks in some snow patches. A little more checking and we found the animal had halted, then turned about and headed away at a steady pace. I couldn't understand this since we were downwind of the animal and we'd been moving especially cautiously. The answer was supplied when we got back to where we'd left the tape machine. In his excitement the lad had allowed the tape to run on beyond the cow calls and instead had played a bull call. We surmised the animal that had answered was a very young bull and probably wanted no part of a fight for the attention of our taped cows!

I suppose there is something to be said for using taped game calls, but I've never used any since, nor been with anyone who has. I figure, as that incident clearly showed, taped calls can be somewhat disastrous and should perhaps be used only by hunters or guides far more dedicated and experienced than myself at accurately mimicking the correct calls, at the correct time. Otherwise a fellow might well be in danger of becoming the inadvertent object of the amorous attentions of a randy bull moose, a consummation devoutly not to be wished!

CHAPTER 10
NEVER CRY FOR THE WOLF

Despite the contentions of those, many of 'em, who've never spent much if any time in the backcountry or listened at length to people who've lived their lives there, the "cry for the wolf" syndrome seems to me to be ninety percent misguided nonsense. The remainder would seem to be misdirected concern. All of those with whom I've spoken on this particular issue, and I might add all have lived their lives in Chilcotin country or other back- and highcountry parts of this province, put no stock whatsoever in the claims and arguments of anti-wolf kill protestors and paraders. These men and women do not deny the wolf has a place in our natural scheme of things, but they also point out that the wolf has to be kept in its place.

We are extremely fortunate in that we have here a very large and most magnificent province into which could be placed the combined American states of Washington, Oregon, Idaho, California and New Mexico and still have land left over. Yet our total population is little more than three millions, while the sum population of those states is more than double that of the whole of Canada. The major portion of BC's population is concentrated in the southwest corner of the province. The wolf ranges fairly freely through much of the rest of it.

If we wish to turn the province or the greater portion of it into a totally pristine wilderness, much as it was before the white man came, fair enough. Such a situation of course is now impossible— just as impossible as British Columbians or, for that matter, the majority of Canadians giving up eating meat. Ergo, we need our cattle ranches and ranges. And the ranches and ranges need to be constantly checked to control the wolf populations therein.

The same must be said of our game populations, at least until or unless a government comes to power that decides to bar entirely all hunting in this province. Somehow I doubt such a policy would ever seriously be entertained let alone be acceptable to a majority of British Columbians, to say nothing of the thousands of tourists who visit the province annually to fish and hunt.

Furthermore, in the face of the preaching and prattling of professional protestors against wolf kills and controls and against trapping (in the latter instance, these misinformed do-gooders would seemingly cheerfully wipe out the livelihood of thousands of Canadians, many of whom are native Indians), I prefer to go with the opinions and experience of those who know whereof they speak— our field conservation officers and biologists, fish and game guides and outfitters, farmers and ranchers—all of whom not only speak from direct experience but also contribute greatly to the economic health and well-being of this province.

Let me give you but two such sources. First Cyril Shelford, of whom I have written earlier and who, by necessity of his livelihood as rancher and guide as well as fisher and hunter, and his many years in public life, speaks from practical experience on the subject of wolves and wolf control. Not elimination, mark you, but sensible, realistic control and balance.

Another source is Eric Collier had it not been for whom, as I also mentioned in an earlier chapter, small and big game and fish would not abound today in the forests, meadows, mountains, lakes and rivers of the Chilcotin. Indeed, were it not for Collier's fight years ago to re-establish the beaver throughout that vast territory, there could well be neither wild game nor fish whatsoever up there.

Both men have pointed out that the wolf is not, repeat NOT, the noble beast and clean killer its apologists, long on theory and woefully short on field craft, would have us believe. Unlike the lioness and lion, the leopard, cheetah, even the grizzly, the wolves kill more in the style of African wild dogs and hyenas. That is, they kill literally in bits and pieces, for the most part biting and slashing away at the bellies, hindquarters and reproductive organs of most game animals and cattle. More often than not, they eat their prey alive, bringing about a slow, obviously painful and terror-stricken death. Wolves have been known and seen to leave a partly-eaten animal to drag itself around for hours before eventually expiring from its wounds, or not until its tormentors' eating finally reaches its vital organs. That is the way of the wolf and thus an integral part of nature's scheme of things. Let me quote here from Eric Collier's *Three Against the Wilderness:*

> ....there was black rage born in my heart, an oath on my lips, the day I stalked broodily around one of our four finest beaver colonies and marked the telltale evidence of the havoc the wolf's penchant for murder had wreaked upon the beavers....There was the offal of one's guts here, a few bedraggled scraps of fur there. There was the half eaten carcass of an old buck beaver alongside a recently felled cottonwood tree, and that was ample indication to me the wolf was full of belly before ever he sank his teeth into that one.
>
> But it was the killing of the old mother beaver that fanned my rage into wild and terrible flame. There she lay, belly to the sun, not more than a dozen steps from the lodge, bloated and stinking, dark underfur speckled with blowfly eggs. She was an old beaver true, but in her very prime where motherhood is concerned. She was an old sow beaver who could be reckoned upon to give birth to four or five sturdy kits each June for many a June to come. But now she was dead, killed by a single crunch of the wolf's rapacious jaws. Yet not an ounce of her flesh had the wolf eaten. Here before me was the wilderness in its sourest mood; a mother beaver killed for no useful purpose whatsoever, at least none that I could think of. (NY: Dutton, 1959)

Some years back when Cyril Shelford was commissioned by the provincial government to study in detail the need for a balanced wolf-control program in British Columbia, he recorded such telling facts as follows: "…although no hunting is allowed in provincial parks such as Tweedsmuir, elk in that park were wiped out, not by disease or winter kill, but, wolves." In this regard also, it is interesting to note a report in an early 1989 issue of *BC Outdoors* magazine:

> Caribou calf survival in the Quesnel Lake junction area is practically nil, claimed Dr. Dale Seip of UBC, who has carried out extensive studies of the herds over the past five years. Attempts to undertake a wolf control program last year (1988) were stopped by conservation groups opposed to the kill. Seip believes that without this control the caribou herds are doomed because of the intensity of wolf predation.
>
> The western woodland caribou is listed by the World Wildlife Fund as a rare species, and both Alberta and the U.S. have upgraded their classification of the animal to 'threatened', a notch above being 'endangered'. The researcher claims time is critical if BC is going to maintain its caribou population. He added that it takes 50 years to bring populations back to reasonable levels, and an immediate wolf control program is a last chance.

In the interview I was fortunate enough to conduct with Eric Collier a few months prior to his death, he opined the best methods of a sound wolf-control program were trapping and/or shooting. On the other hand, Shelford and I part company on his ideas for such control, poisoning, but not that I feel so much for the wolf in such circumstances. Rather I believe this can set off a dangerous and sometimes irreversible chain of events. For example, a poisoned wolf carcass can pass along the poison to animal and bird scavengers. I therefore hew to Collier's contention, believing the less dangerous idea is to trap and/or shoot. A realistic bounty would be of great benefit, too, to trappers as well as ranchers and farmers.

I well recall Joe Schuk setting his own bounty a few years back of fifty dollars a wolf. He placed a hand-printed notice to that effect on a tree on the south side of the bridge at Henry's Crossing. I still have a picture I took of the notice at the time. Joe did this at the height of a BC-wide wolf-kill controversy when, you may remember, a covey of Lower Mainland and imported professional protestors from the U.S. gave up their stated intention to follow and harass hunting parties in the far north of this province, after starting out with the usual hyped-up television and print propaganda. Apparently the weather was too cold and their knowledge of wilderness survival was sadly lacking—a dismal admission, perhaps, that there is a great difference between fact and fiction, theory and practise.

Incidentally, Joe never did have to pay up. The wolf, after all, is a somewhat smarter animal than the average hunter and backcountry visitor, and even seasoned guides and trappers at times. Or it could be, as some of its apologists might have us believe, that the wolf can read in one, if not both, official languages!

I will say when the quiet of a highcountry night is broken by the call of wolves, as I have often heard across lakes or back in the timber from our camp, it is an integral part of that world I do not wish to see disappear entirely. In some respects, perhaps, it is an opus of nature's symphony without which the whole would be sadly lacking.

A log dropped in the stove firebox bringing me sharply out of my reverie. I glanced at my watch and realised it was almost midnight. The quarter moon shone into the cabin, its reflection now dappled on the lake surface, as a slight breeze had risen. It was also much cooler inside the cabin. As I stoked up the stove again and set the damper lever to its lowest, it was as if the Almighty had been privy to my mental wanderings because, at that moment, from the other side of the lake came a wolf call. Within seconds the cry was taken up by another wolf, and it soon became evident there was a small pack of five or six animals trailing something across there in the timber.

Having completed my stoking chore, I climbed into my sleeping bag and was beginning to drift off when I heard a scuttering across the floor. A mouse, doubtless an established resident of the cabin, probably figured that, now that two-legged intruder had turned in for the night, it was time for him, or her, to scout for something edible. I leaned down from my perch, grabbed a boot and threw it at the wee scutterer, which promptly popped down a hole in the floorboards. Perhaps it was poetic justice of a sort since I had made that particular hole on a previous stay in the Far Meadow cabin....

CHAPTER 11
ACCIDENTS WILL HAPPEN

I was introducing two more old friends to Chilcotin country when I accidentally put the hole in the floor of the Far Meadow cabin.

Rod Heinekey at the time was a "Seafairy": more accurately, a member of the Seafarers' Union. I'd known Heinekey, if anything, longer than my other old former SIU friend, Alf Poole. After Rod learned I'd taken Poole up into that backcountry, he extracted a promise from me that one year I'd take him up there. Came the time when I fulfilled my promise. With us on that trip was Bob Stradling, a longtime photographer friend. Stradling was not only a newcomer to the Chilcotin; it was also his first ever hunting trip. But, true to his profession, he hunted with camera. As it turned out, he was more successful than Heinekey or myself. We didn't get any big game. Stradling, however, shot numerous excellent pictures throughout the trip—pictures that made my photographic efforts look precisely what they were, amateurish by comparison. Nevertheless, it was another most enjoyable trip.

We'd been at the Far Meadow cabin a couple of days when the hole in the floor incident occurred. We'd finished dinner. The dishes were washed and stacked. The other two were sitting at the table on the far side of the cabin having a spirituous nightcap. I was checking out a recently acquired handgun, a short-barreled .357 magnum. Following time-honoured police practise, I had put five shells into the cylinder, leaving one chamber empty. Why I had loaded the weapon at all, even in that fashion, I really don't know. Anyway, I followed procedure by lining up the empty chamber with the barrel.

97

However, it was once again what the Tigger often describes when I become forgetful, a case of "old-timer's disease"! The correct process is to have the empty chamber to one side or other of the chamber that is lined up with the barrel. Then when the trigger is pressed and the cylinder revolves, the empty chamber is lined up. The trigger is pressed and the firing pin merely clicks forward into that empty space. Or that's the way it should be. In my case it wasn't. Pointing the weapon downward, I pressed the trigger and WHAM....

The sound of a .357 magnum fired in the confines of that cabin certainly startled me. The effect on Stradling and Heinekey was something else again. Rod was about to take a sip, and as I looked over, I swear the liquid was suspended in air, midway between the glass itself and the ceiling. Stradling, normally pale of complexion, seemed a few shades paler.

Once both realised I hadn't done myself irreparable injury, both of 'em recited the history of my ancestors in less than drawing-room terms. Some weeks after we returned home, Rod's wife, a lady of wicked wit, told us, "It took me a month to get the brown stain out of his [Rod's] underwear after that trip."

The day we came out on that same trip, I decided to take the old road once we were over the river at Henry's Crossing. It's about a forty-mile stretch along that road to Alexis Creek. When I first started going into Chilcotin country, we'd often take the same road, which for much of that forty miles parallels the river. In those days, it was best described in Joe Schuk's way as, "A good road, but a slow road." It used to take about eight hours to travel that distance. Now one can do it in less than three.

When I took Stradling and Heinekey along there, we left the Crossing shortly after noon, and I reckoned we'd be at Alexis Creek mid, or at most late, afternoon. Unfortunately, about the halfway mark, the springs on the left side of the trailer gave way. We were able to block the body of the trailer clear of the axle with a piece of wood, but it meant we couldn't make more than five or six miles an hour. Thus we didn't pull into Alexis until early evening. In turn, that meant a call to the Red Coach Inn at 100 Mile House, where I'd previously arranged we would overnight before heading back home.

I had also made reservations for dinner in what I've long considered one of the finest dining rooms anywhere in this province, The Burghley Room at the Inn. Despite the slowdown caused by the problem with the trailer, I reckoned that after the accommodating fellow at the lone Alexis Creek gas station performed a quick spot-welding job, we'd be down at the 100 in time for dinner before the dining room closed, usually nine p.m. week nights.

It didn't work out quite as planned. We reached the top of the hill just east of Lee's Corner, and the spot-weld gave out. By then, however, we were back on pavement; so after once again blocking up the bed of the trailer, we were able to make good time.

We were on the main highway about ten miles south of Williams Lake travelling at the posted speed of fifty-five. I was driving, Heinekey was in the passenger seat beside me, and Stradling in the rear. Suddenly the right rear tire of the Jimmy literally blew. I never found out whether the "brown stain" to which Rod's wife subsequently referred derived from the hole-in-the-floor episode or from the blown-tire incident. Suffice to say, the anal orifices of all three of us were unusually tight for the minutes it took me to wrestle the vehicle off to the side of the highway, coming from 55 mph to a full stop without yawing all over the pavement, much less being rear-ended by a following vehicle.

By the time we changed the wheel and arrived at the Inn it was after ten o'clock. It was then that my partners experienced the incomparable courtesy and hospitality of that establishment. Despite the fact the dining room had been closed, the hostess, Miss Karen Barger, and the front desk receptionist had stayed beyond their normal end of shift awaiting our safe arrival. They hadn't heard from us, of course, since I had phoned some four hours earlier from Alexis Creek.

Prior to going up to our rooms, Miss Barger asked if we'd like sandwiches and coffee sent up, to which I said yes. We hadn't been in the rooms more than a few minutes when the phone rang. The same young lady informed us that the senior chef, another female, said she had nothing planned for the rest of that evening, and if we wished, she'd willingly make what she called a "proper meal" for three fellows just back from the bush. She didn't consider sandwiches met that criterion. Ergo, we were later served a full-course dinner. That is true hospitality.

When the Red Coach Inn opened in 1966, I was fortunate enough to spend the first of what, over intervening years, have been many nights in that hostelry. My first evening was unscheduled. In the spring of that year I also met for the first time the man who, in large measure, was responsible for the design and decor of the Inn, Max von Hartman. Another post WWII immigrant, Max came to Canada from Germany in the mid-fifties. A former German paratrooper, he had been captured by our side in the latter months of the war and spent the next months, until the fighting ended, in an Allied prison camp.

When I met von Hartman that spring, he invited me to visit the Inn on my way up hunting that fall. In addition to laying out the basic design and colour scheme for the Inn, for the first ten years of its operation, he was manager and senior chef. I was always of the opinion he set up the best stocked bar anywhere in BC those early years of Red Coach operation.

When we got up there that fall, the nephew of one of my partners, then living in 100 Mile House and who held a pilot's license, had arranged to rent an aircraft in which he, his uncle and myself were to fly over the country where we were to hunt. At the last minute, however, I backed down since I wished to overnight at the Inn and spend the next morning with Max, touring the establishment. Another partner, a doctor of naturopathy from the Lower Mainland, was to join us around noon at the Inn, he having had to leave the morning after we left home base.

Following my guided tour, von Hartman and I were starting lunch when I spotted the doctor across the way just finishing his meal. After the introductions, the doctor, true to his naturopathic bent, waxed ecstatic about the food. He became more enthused when von Hartman explained that the bread came from the Red Coach bakery, the meat from organically fed cattle, and the vegetables were also organically grown. That brought from the physician a glowing tribute for the vegetable soup with which he'd started his lunch. In turn that gave Max an opening to tell a classic story.

"The same year the Inn opened," Max began, "so did a new 100 Mile House hospital. As with all government underwritten projects, the hospital had been planned a decade earlier, based on the area population of that time. This resulted in bed shortages on occasion. And on one such occasion a Chilcotin rancher en route to Vancouver decided to try the much-talked-about hospitality of our Inn. Prior to dinner he downed a few glasses of conviviality. As he was seated for dinner, the waitress tried a number of times to get him to try the vegetable soup. Well, the rancher wasn't interested. The girl persisted to the point where the rancher was ready to walk out without dinner. Finally he prevailed on the young woman to forget the soup.

"After finishing his soupless dinner, he enjoyed more liquid libation in the bar, then went to bed. In keeping with an arrangement between the new hospital and the Inn, a man was brought to the Inn who was scheduled for an appendectomy the following day. There was a shortage of beds at the hospital, and the patient was settled in a room next to the rancher's. Shortly thereafter, the duty sister came over from the hospital to give the patient an enema. Seeing no one at the hotel desk, under the same standing arrangement she took the room key, went upstairs and administered the enema to the semi-comatose patient in the prescribed manner.

"Some weeks later a friend of the rancher, intending to visit the coast, asked about accommodations *et al* at the Inn. The rancher told him it was indeed an excellent establishment. Very reasonable rates. No parking problems. Courteous service and incomparably good food.

"'But,' he warned, 'if they try to sell you soup with dinner, for God's sake, take it. If you don't, they'll shove it up your ass at one in the morning!'

"Transpired the duty sister had entered the wrong room and given the wrong man the enema. The ultimate fate of the legitimate patient remains unknown."

In the years since, whenever I overnighted at the Inn, I continued to enjoy the unrivalled hospitality and food but never, fortunately, had soup served in that unique fashion in the wee small hours!

For a number of years the Inn was entirely owned and operated by the semi-religious group that also, until fairly recently, pretty well owned 100 Mile House itself. The group was started by a man known for decades as the Bishop of the Cariboo, Lord Martin Cecil, Marquess of Exeter. His family had owned the lands in that area for many years previously, which is why the official name of the town still shown on the railroad signs up there is Exeter, not 100 Mile House. Martin came out in the twenties and, as well as managing and expanding the Bridge Creek ranch, he literally built much of the town. The family also owned most of the town properties, which resulted in businesses and residences being built to a specific standard laid down by Martin—in some respect what might be considered a sort of feudal but generally beneficial system.

More recently, the Cecils relinquished much of their original town holdings. Martin died in 1988. His son, Michael, whose aircraft my partner and his nephew rented that first time at the Inn, has since succeeded to the title and lands.

I interviewed Martin a number of times prior to his death and on occasion engaged in some spirited but pleasant discussion on the makeup, background and philosophy of the group whose creed is Ontology, and which calls itself the Emissaries of Divine Light. Its main tenet equates God with Nature and vice versa. Being something of an inveterate sinner myself, I've always been interested in what the "other side," so to speak, does and thinks.

In the realm of accidents there have been others on our trips. Looking back on them, once one has survived the problem, each in its own way adds to the retrospective enjoyment of our journeys. At the time, however, as in the case of the trailer breakdown and the tire exploding on the highway, they are anything but welcome.

There was the time, as Dan and I were coming out after a couple of weeks up country, when the lad, then seventeen or eighteen, got me all the way from the Timothy Meadow camp to about a quarter of a mile from a service station in Williams Lake just as the place was about to close for the night. It was full dark, a little after eight of a November evening. I had literally coasted the Jimmy all the way down the hill on Highway 20 into the town proper, without lights. Everything else on the vehicle was dying a slow death. The alternator was on its last legs. Point of fact, it had been dying for some hours, but I hadn't realised the precise problem.

The first indication of trouble came when we left Timothy Meadow. It was snowing lightly, but by the time we reached Joe Schuk's home ranch, the snow had stopped. Cliff and Cal were there also, and between them and the Tigger, they figured the battery was going. They charged it up and away we went. We got as far as Redstone before charging up again. By then Dan figured we may not need a new battery so much as a new alternator. However, we managed to get to the place as I mentioned atop the hill before Williams Lake before the lights went. When we reached the bottom of the hill, everything expired. Dan ran uphill to the only service station still seemingly operating, one that was about to close. He got the proprietor to drive down to where the Jimmy, trailer and I were marooned and install the new battery, and we were away.

Next morning at the Red Coach, while I was still showering, Dan was up and out. He took the vehicle to the nearest service station, made a deal with that operator to trade the old alternator for a new one, with a reasonable discount on the trade, then installed the new one himself in no time flat, and it's been there ever since.

The Tigger was also with me when I blew a hole in the roof of the Jimmy. We were spending a few days with Aaron Raboff and his wife at their Rangeland ranch, which extends from just south and east of Lone Butte down to Green Lake. Dan was using my rifle and I in turn had one from another friend living up there. We had just returned from an afternoon's leisurely and unsuccessful hunt through part of Aaron's property. As the young fellow got out of the vehicle, he cleared the weapon and handed it to me, bolt open, as I sat in the Jimmy. I closed the bolt and, as is my practise, holding the weapon upright, I pressed the trigger.

The sound of a .303 inside a vehicle is if anything noisier than a .357 fired in a highcountry cabin. As Dan approached the house, Mrs. Raboff came to the door and asked, "Did you get anything?"

Dan replied in his usually dry, laconic manner, "Yes, my dad just shot the Jimmy!"

He had cleared the magazine all right, but a shell had become lodged in the breech.

Only two or three years ago when Dan first spent time at Chaunigan Lake with another unforgettable character living up there, Julien Patenaude, I attempted in effect to fit a square peg in a round hole, or something similar. Shortly after we reached Julien's comfortable lakeshore camp, the Tigger took off with a friend of the Frenchman's to familiarize himself with the territory. Julien and I stayed behind preparing dinner. More precisely, the Frenchman prepared the meal, he being one helluva cook. I offered suggestions, which he studiously ignored while I sipped my evening olive soup. When darkness fell, the others hadn't returned. I became worried because of course Dan didn't know that country at all and Julien's friend wasn't very familiar with the area either, according to the Frenchman. After an hour or so, we both became very concerned. I went outside to fire off a few rounds from my twelve gauge. Imagine my surprise when the shells I placed in both barrels simply slipped down into the barrels.

I had picked up a box of twenty-gauge shells. In fact I had done that as we left home. A twelve-gauge gun doesn't operate too well with twenty-gauge shells—another example of "old-timer's disease." Moments later, both wanderers returned unhurried and unconcerned.

It was on the same trip that Julien and I roared away from the little dock he'd built to do some afternoon fishing. We were set up shortly thereafter and as I was about to light a pipe, damned if a fish didn't hit my line. With hook well set I started reeling in. It took about twenty minutes to bring a decent-sized fish close to the boat, and the Frenchman looked around for the net. We had left the ruddy thing on the dock!

Nothing ventured, nothing gained. I took a chance and yanked the fish out of the water and into the boat. It was indeed a "lucky strike"—a healthy rainbow between four and five pounds. As soon as it was boated, we sped back to pick up the net then resumed fishing. That was the only fish we caught that afternoon.

I've had a twelve-foot aluminum boat and small Evinrude motor for a dozen or more years. Most of the early years, however, I rarely got the chance to use it, so I loaned boat and motor to an RCMP friend when he was transferred from Lower Mainland duties to Kamloops. For the next two or three years he, his wife and daughter got well and truly into fishing in and around there. One of those summers my lass and I went to spend a few days with them. Wilf Studer and I took off the first full day up there to try our luck. We got the boat in the water and the motor in place. And for the next ten or fifteen minutes, I tried repeatedly, without success, to get that motor started. After listening to my cursing and blinding, Studer looked over and gently suggested it might make a difference if I turned the throttle to *Start*. I didn't have my spectacles with me and not having used the boat much prior to loaning it to them, I had suffered still another bout of "old-timer's."

Later that year, Slack, Dan and I arranged to have the Studers meet us at Cache Creek, where we'd pick up the boat to take on that year's hunt, the Studers having by then purchased their own boat and motor.

A few days later, I put the boat in at our Taylor Lake campsite. As I clamped the motor on, I noticed a piece of paper taped to the cover. On it, written in Cathy (Cookie) Studer's neat hand was the admonition, "To start, turn to *Start*." Such is the lack of respect for age and attendant infirmities of us older citizens from some young women nowadays!

Chaunigan Lake is a body of glacier-fed water, five thousand feet up on the eastern edge of the Coast Range. It is about three miles long and a mile or so at its widest point. The fishing is excellent, particularly if M. Patenaude is along. He spends much of the year up there and has built a small, but extremely comfortable, camp on the north shore near the western end of the lake. I swear by all the gods, that damnable Frenchman puts crosses on the lake water because he rarely goes out but what he doesn't catch fish. Either that, or he talks to the fish. I still haven't learned the language, much less seen the crosses.

On one occasion meantime, he and Dan were building a porch and a shower stall onto the main cabin. It's a measure of Julien's bush carpentry and construction expertise that after the shower stall was built a pleasantly warm shower can be enjoyed at any time. He runs a pipe from the sixty-gallon tank built into the rafters of the cabin. The heat from the stove heats not only the cabin but also the water in the tank, and there you have it—a warm shower.

While those two were busy at the shower and porch project, Julien asked, in his somewhat fragmented English, if I would fetch some "tin wood" from a pile of material some distance back in the trees. I returned shortly with some sheets of tin I'd found back there. Both the Tigger and the Frenchman looked at each other, then at me as though I were at least three or four bricks short of a load. What Julien had meant was for me to bring over a load of "thin" pieces of wood, something like elongated shakes, for the roof of the porch and shower stall. But as I say, his English often loses something in the interpretation, thus "thin" wood in his lexicon becomes "tin" wood.

When he becomes annoyed, however, Julien abandons English for his first language. This was evidenced once when we three took a day to make the circuit from his lake campsite, up over a nearby ridge, then down across the Taseko River, on to Lee's Corner, west through Alexis Creek, Redstone, Tatla Lake and on to visit the Schuks. We hadn't left camp more than half an hour when Julien, riding with me in the Jimmy, explained how I must turn the vehicle sharply left to avoid a large, deep mudhole. To make things more interesting, a big tree root jutted out into the trail. It was a case of swinging the wheels to starboard to get around the root, then sharply to port to avoid the hole and stay on the trail. I made the right turn well enough, but as I switched left, I struck the root, which was greasier than usual due to recent heavy showers.

Into the hole slid the front of the Jimmy. Julien resorted to French to vent his feelings toward me and my driving. I verbally bludgeoned him in English. As we got out and started digging, Dan, who had been following on foot, sauntered up, listened and watched for a while. Then, grinning in that puckish fashion he uses whenever he takes a verbal jab at his old man, remarked, "Don't forget, you have a winch on the front of the Jimmy." That was an instance where both M. Patnaude and myself suffered an attack of that disease, both having momentarily forgotten we did have the winch.

Aided by a nearby stump, we were out of the hole and on our way in five minutes. For quite a while thereafter, neither of us said a word; but behind us, as he walked along, I'm sure I heard the Tigger chuckling away to himself.

I suppose the main point about this chapter is, a man can prepare for almost anything and still be caught out. Yet the gods seem to have pity on us and eventually smile. And, I repeat, such incidents make for more interesting trips and give a fellow something to yarn about long afterward. Personally, I wouldn't miss it for the world, and as the Tigger printed on a plaque many years ago while still in grade school and that now hangs in our kitchen:

I love the Fall, the grass is green,
such colours I have never seen.
I love the Fall, the air is sweet,
and everything has dancing feet,
In lovely Fall.

"Tigger" & "Jax" on left in Chilcotin country circa 1990s

CHAPTER 12
THE 4 S's and THE LADY SAYS NO

"Shit, Shave, Shower and Shampoo" is a maxim of military service that could be construed as unwritten holy writ—a ritual with which one started the day whenever and wherever possible. During my days behind barbed wire, it was a vitally necessary ritual for the sake of one's health and overall well-being, as well as a great morale booster.

On hunting and fishing trips, it is a ritual, I have to confess, to which I've not always strictly adhered. Not daily insofar as the latter three components are concerned. I have invariably succeeded in performing daily ablutions via early morning stripped to the waist washing, a much more enjoyable task in a camper or cabin but even outside when neither of those are always available. Shaving upcountry is never indulged in until the day we leave for home. I have made use of the shower installed at Patenaude's Chaunigan Lake camp and thoroughly enjoyed it. I have also taken more than one plunge into that lake. While the initial shock of immersing in glacier water tends to shrivel one's family jewels and (thank providence I am now retired from broadcasting) raise the voice a couple of octaves, such plunges are most refreshing.

The Tigger has taken numerous dips in Chaunigan, Taylor and other highcountry lakes and survived none the worse for them. In fact, at least once during almost every trip, he's made with me, he bathes and shampoos in all but below zero weather.

Thinking back on these things brings to what I choose to call my mind one of the many most amusing incidents from the days behind the wire. This occurred in the camp at Stargard where, as earlier pointed out, we Canadian "schwein" had been gathered together for that "preferential treatment" go round.

One morning in late spring 1944, word came from the camp commandant's office that a top-ranked German brass hat was going to visit the camp later that day. Together with that information we were told, since that idiotic exercise in futility was still officially on the books, we Canadians must wear handcuffs for the duration of the visit to our compound.

Apparently there was a helluva scramble among the commandant's staff because initially no one seemed to know where the manacles were stored. Thereafter, they weren't sure if they had enough of 'em to go around! When the Canadian contingent was first assembled at the Stargard camp, the Germans began the handcuffing caper all over again, but it hadn't lasted long. They soon tired of it, and as happened in the first days it was in vogue a few months after the Dieppe show, the amount of cuffs handed out each morning never matched the amount collected at the end of those days.

As it turned out, the Germans at Stargard managed to come up with enough pairs to cuff most of us before the visiting brass hat arrived. He was Sepp Dietrich, at that point still one of Hitler's favourite generals. Despite that, Dietrich was also one of the brightest and shrewdest armoured warfare tacticians the Germans had. Many on our side ranked him with Guderian, von Kleist and even the fabled Rommel.

Our official greeting party was composed of a British medical officer, a Captain Taverner, who together with a competent Germany army medical officer operated the camp hospital; our senior warrant officer, Sergeant Major Tony Anthony, also our compound leader in dealings with the commandant and his staff; a fellow from the South Saskatchewans whose name now escapes me, who was of German extraction, and myself as interpreters. The German retinue was about a dozen strong, including the camp commandant and his interpreter and the officer in charge of our compound, Hauptmann (Captain) Hauffe. He incidentally was one of the very few Germans who escaped from a prisoner of war camp in Britain during the First World War, a feat for which he was awarded the Knight's Order of the Iron Cross.

The barrack blocks in the compounds in that camp housing prisoners of various nationalities, including us, were built in sections of two blocks, each housing in excess of one hundred men in three tier bunks. Each two-barrack block was joined in the centre by a bathhouse. There were no showers. Instead, each bathhouse contained half a dozen long metal troughs. Above each trough was a water pipe, and every couple of feet along the separate sections of pipe were taps. The water, of course, was cold. Whenever a fellow wished to shower or do laundry that was the place for it. A somewhat primitive system, but it worked fairly well.

As the official party was walking through the first barrack block, a fellow named Jimmy Donald from my regiment and that of Tony Anthony, the Royal Regiment, was in the connecting bathhouse stripped to the buff, taking a stand-up bath. I happened to be ahead of the official party passing word of their approach. As I walked through the bathhouse, there was Donald busy at his ablutions. Hanging over the water pipe in front of him was a pair of handcuffs. I returned to the upper barrack block in time to following the German party as they stepped into the bathhouse. In those few interim seconds, Donald had put on the handcuffs and was standing stiffly to attention in the far corner of the room as the general and party walked through. Dietrich acknowledged Donald with a peremptory salute, walked a few paces farther, then stopped, turned, and for all of ten seconds studied Donald, obviously trying to figure out how the devil this ball-naked prisoner managed to remove his clothes without removing the manacles! It was a fascinating tableau: one of the great panzer generals the Germans had during the Second World War puzzling out that question. Suddenly the light dawned, and he ordered one of his underlings to take Jimmy's name and POW number. Donald was to be sent down to the punishment cells for a seven-day stretch as soon as the visit was over.

An hour or so later, however, as the German party was leaving our compound, Dietrich turned to us for a final few words. And as he returned our salutes he grinned, turned to the earlier mentioned underling and said, "Remove that man's name from your book. He deserves to get away with it!" Jimmy Donald, who after the war joined the Toronto police force, did not go into the cooler that day in the spring of 1944. Later that same day, however, when all the gold-braided brass hats had left and guards came in to collect the manacles, they recovered less than half the number they'd distributed. I believe Donald was one, and I know Tony Anthony and myself among others, who had swiped a pair. For many months after I returned to Canada, I kept those handcuffs and often during liquid lubricated lie-swapping sessions with friends would bring 'em out and retell the story of the time a frontline Canadian soldier momentarily flummoxed the great Dietrich.

On the subject once again of cold water bathing in Chilcotin lakes and creeks, Roy Slack took a plunge one day in late October in Taylor Lake. Fact is, he went whole hog, doing his laundry and taking a bath at the same time. He went in fully clothed, although it wasn't exactly planned that way.

Slack, like Julien Patenaude, the Schuks and almost all high country residents, and in some measure my errant son, is something of a jack-of-all-trades. On the hunting trip in question, one of the batteries in my Jimmy became tilted on a particularly rough trek. Much of the fluid in the battery was spilled, something that went unnoticed for a couple of days until I chanced to check the oil level. Slack set to work, painstakingly straining water from the lake through a piece of cheesecloth. Shortly before dinner was ready and the evening's batch of martinis mixed and cooling in a thermos tied to a branch over the edge of the lake, he finished the job and was in the process of washing in the lake when I heard him give out with a sound like a combination of a yell and a high-pitched shriek. He'd fallen into the water.

As he scrambled out and headed for the camper, I called to him to "hold it." He obligingly did, standing there dripping wet while I shot a picture of him in his sorry and shivering state. I've often since thought this was a true indication of friendship. I'm sure had it been anyone else, I would have been told exactly where to put my camera and how far up!

After he'd stripped to the skin and taken a standup bath (with warm water inside the camper), Slack hung his wet duds on a nearby tree. Next morning they were stiff as boards, the overnight temperature having fallen well below freezing. The evening of his plunge, I doubled his olive soup ration. I figured I owed him!

One of the more unusual incidents to do with stream and lake bathing, voluntary and otherwise, featured the Tigger and Solo, the latter being a Black Lab retriever belonging to Rod Heinekey. It was Heinekey's second trip with me. Stradling wasn't along that time, but Dan was. We were comfortably settled in the Timothy Lake cabin. It was early November and, although the days were clear and warm, the nights were frosty.

The young fellow and Solo formed a firm friendship from the start of the trip. One of the games they played was for the Tigger to throw small rocks into an adjacent branch of Brittany Creek to roust small fish, and the dog would jump in trying to catch one. Despite his being an excellent bird dog, Solo never mastered fishing, but the game was obviously great fun for both.

One evening following dinner and after what had now become a nightly routine, the dog, having dutifully shaken off excess creek water, was stretched out by the stove. Dan, a lifelong dog lover, figured Solo needed extra warmth. To the eyebrow-cocked amusement of Heinekey and myself, the Tigger threw his still fairly new woolen jacket over the animal. The remainder of the trip Solo slept each night, by the stove, covered with that jacket.

One summer years ago, I made a gross error in judgment. I took the woman I have long referred to as She who must be obeyed, Her Royal Highness, even on occasion less complimentary titles, into the Chilcotin.

From the start she wasn't all that enthusiastic, but I had propagandized her for some considerable time about the magnificence of the area, and I suppose she ultimately decided, best get it over with once and for all. So, away we went the weekend of the

113

BC Day holiday that year. In those days I didn't have a camper, so we travelled in the Jimmy, HRH riding alongside me, Dan and his sister Andrea in the back. In some respects, not having a camper compounded my initial error. It may have been somewhat crowded, more so certainly than SWMBO would have liked, but it would not have necessitated our spending the first night of the holiday at the Red Coach Inn. The comfort of that establishment merely served to highlight our subsequent time in the backcountry.

The first full day out from the Inn we took our time to Williams Lake, then west, and broke for lunch at the lookout above Lee's Corner. To that point, things were going reasonably well.

A second error on my part had been to invite along a couple who had their own vehicle, who claimed to enjoy the backwoods, but as it turned out, there was more fiction than fact to that claim.

I should point out here that, at the time of that trip, the paved section of highway twenty west of Williams Lake ended at Lee's Corner. This meant the major portion of the journey into highcountry was by gravel road—a good road sure enough, but gravel roads at the height of summer, and that turned out to be the hottest day of that summer, are not the best for a suburban born and raised lady to travel. More so since, in addition to the dust, a couple of cantankerous kids in the same vehicle did not enhance the journey. I broke our journey at Alexis Creek to check in with an old friend, Sergeant Mike Hewatt, OC of the Queen's Cowboy detachment.

"How long will you be out?" Mike asked. It was then Monday.

Vaguely, I replied, "Saturday or possibly Friday."

"Well," he said, checking out our travelling party, "if I haven't heard from you by Sunday, we'll send out the dogs!"

Beyond Alexis I turned onto the old river road. It was much slower going than the main road but less dusty and cooler because much of the road is tree lined or trees overhang the road. By late afternoon, we were close to Henry's Crossing and the young'uns had settled down fairly well, although my lass, I noticed, was not her usually communicative self any longer.

I halted to check the staples and other items we were hauling in the trailer. That was when I discovered another absolutely ludicrous mistake on my part. For some, even to this day, inexplicable reason, I had packed our supply of liquid conviviality in with the potatoes, other vegetables and canned goods. Clearly I had not packed the martini mixings nearly well enough. The bottles had cracked, and though my lady and I didn't have martinis the remainder of the time, I must confess our potatoes and other vegetables were the tastiest I've ever eaten, garnished as they were with gin and vermouth.

Despite this bitter blow, we pressed on to and across the river, thence at an even slower pace, given the road condition, toward the Timothy Meadow cabin where I hoped we could spend the night.

It usually takes about an hour to drive the ten or twelve miles from the bridge to Timothy. The sun was now sinking slowly behind the trees. There was no dust to speak of, and the cool of evening was upon us. The offspring now were absolutely quiet. So was Lila. Ominously so. Hadn't said one word since we crossed the river. I broke the silence with the observation, "You know, lass, you've often heard me say one of the reasons I so love this country is because so very few people come through here." That was a very grave error indeed. She whom I have known and loved for more than thirty years reacted in a fashion that startled me so much I damned near drove off the road. Not until that point in all our time together hitherto did I realise she knew so many rousing expletives. "Who..." she began, increasing her volume as she continued, "who in their [expletive deleted] right [expletive deleted] mind would [expletive deleted] want to come into this [expletive deleted] country, especially at this [expletive deleted] time of year!"

She then subsided into a taut and dignified silence—a silence I sensibly decided not to break.

When we reached the cabin all of us descended wordlessly from our vehicle into two-foot high grass. Both Andrea and her Mum were wearing slacks, and a myriad of tiny flying creatures invaded their nether limbs. Lila's silence was now at the pregnant point where it could be most acutely felt. It didn't last long. As I led her into the cabin where her son, her spouse and numerous friends have spent many, many comfortable and happy hours, she spotted a plump packrat. It was quite dead in a trap. That, however, did not improve the hour one iota. I reckon she spent all of thirty seconds in the cabin before turning sharply on her heel and storming out and back into the Jimmy. I knew we would not be staying in the cabin this trip.

We drove back to the river. There, under a warm brightly moonlit sky I put up a tent. The youngest of our brood, Andrea, and I bedded down. Dan elected to sleep in the back of the vehicle. HRH sat stonily silent in the front seat. I later learned she slept, but fitfully.

With the break of day she was still regally enthroned there, and I give you my solemn word, she never uttered one word until I'd prepared breakfast and poured her first cup of coffee. That, and a cigarette, produced a slight thaw when she allowed as how it had been an admittedly beautiful night with the moonlight on the fast-flowing river waters and a slight wind stirring the trees.

I should interject here to state that while there was much reason for her initial reactions given her suburban upbringing and background, the other couple had beefed and bellyached almost incessantly since we'd crossed the river the night previous.

After breakfast a further check of the supplies in the trailer revealed almost all the labels on the canned goods had been washed away by gin and vermouth—undoubtedly the most exotic and expensive detergent ever devised. In addition, my having to make meals with mystery ingredients removed camp cooking from the ordinary.

Later that morning I shepherded my flock along to Taylor Lake, where we stayed for the next couple of days. By then my lady had returned to her near normally amiable self—even went so far as to say she thought it was quite pleasant there by the lake. Except...

The exception, I realise in retrospect, was a most telling one for females of the species human, particularly those unused to the joys of the great outdoors, more so when camped alongside a mountain lake at the height of summer. The minute flying creatures to which my two gals were introduced at Timothy Meadow were a rude enough introduction to the highcountry, but the mosquitoes, no-see-ums and other pesky predators that feasted on their more curvaceous and tender parts when either, or both, repaired to the tall timber to perform necessary natural functions left not only an indelible, but also a very painful, impression on their flesh and minds. They suffered so many bites and stings, I really believe they contracted a mild, definitely irritating as well as painful, poisoning of their systems.

When we trekked out midweek, both had had more than their fill of the adventure. In turn, I had pretty well had it with the other couple, whose whining and bitching made the attitude and actions of both our young'uns look like hardy pioneers by comparison.

There was one final, more annoying than agonizing, experience for my women. By the time we reached Alexis Creek on the way out, even though I took the upper, faster and more utilized route, their hair stood up from their heads like that of the fabled Sudanese Fuzzy-Wuzzies of Omdurman. Their tresses were literally choked with the fine white dust that is an integral part of travel in and through Chilcotin country when the weather is dry. When I dropped in again to report to Mike Hewatt late that last day, he looked startled.

"What the hell happened?" he began. Before I could answer, he glanced out the window, turned back to me and remarked, "Ah, yes, the ladies. I quite understand."

Our return that evening to the Red Coach was greeted with broad smiles by HRH and Miss Thimbles, as her brother was want to call Andrea in those days when her pubescent contours were only then starting to show her femininity. The prospect of shower, shampoo and a truly gourmet dinner in the Burghley Room made both females realise all was once more well with the world.

In the years since, neither has evidenced any desire whatsoever to go up country again. As Lila succinctly put it, "Once was enough. I've been and seen, and I will be quite satisfied never to do it again."

Of course I might have suggested they both should have taken at least one plunge in Taylor Lake to rid themselves of dust and grime, ease the pain of bites and stings and generally refresh themselves. But then again, I might not still be alive to recount the story to you.

Brandenburg Gate view into East Berlin prior to "fall of the wall"

CHAPTER 13
LET THE CHIPS FALL...

The sun was up but hadn't yet cleared the trees on the eastern shore of the lake at Far Meadow by the time I awakened. It was still fairly warm in the cabin, but when I checked the fire was almost out. After getting it going again, adding a couple more handfuls of coffee to my smoke-blackened pot and setting it on the stove, I pulled on pants and socks, donned a sweater, stuck feet into boots and stepped out to relieve my burdened bladder and greet the day.

The morning was clear and fresh, decidedly so. Frost on the meadow grass sparkled and flashed, jewel-like in the first rays of sunshine now edging over the trees. Ice had begun to form at the lake edges overnight. After paying tribute to the new day and leaving my mark in a clump of now no-longer-frosted grass a few yards from the cabin, I nipped smartly back inside to start breakfast.

Halfway through my small stack of pancakes, as I sat by the window on the west side of the cabin looking over the meadow and the creek as it wound through the middle, I watched a drama begin to unfold. A chapter from the book of everyday wilderness life was about to be written. A mule deer doe emerged from the trees on the far side of the meadow. Behind her trotted a fawn. Judging by its size and the way it was jumping stiff-legged around its mother, it was a few months old and must have been born that spring. A few yards closer to the lake there was a sudden slight movement in the grass at the edge of the meadow on the same side from where the doe and fawn had moved out of the trees.

As the fawn sprang ahead of the doe, intent on its play, the mother raised her head, ears flicking back and forth. The movement in the grass stopped. I couldn't see anything at that point, but it was clear there was something there. I studied the two deer through field glasses then focused on the spot where I'd seen the earlier movement. But I still couldn't see what made the movement. The distance between that point and the doe and fawn was about fifty yards. As they neared a bend in the creek, there was another stealthy movement much closer to them. This time, however, the movement continued, and when I turned the glasses there, I could just see the top of the head and upright, pointed ears of a bobcat. The doe was much too big for the cat to bring down, so it was clear that its target would be the fawn.

The doe and fawn were now close enough to jump the creek when the bobcat made its move. It sprang from its crouch and bounded straight for the fawn. I'm told at flat-out speed, the bobcat can equal the cougar's thirty to forty miles an hour, and this cat was in high gear in seconds. There was a bleating cry of warning from the doe. The fawn was over the creek in a flash, but instead of jumping across herself, the doe swung right around to face the cat. In almost the same movement, she lowered her head and charged the cat. This must have startled the cat because it turned from the direction of the fawn toward the mother and faltered in mid-stride. As the doe continued her charge, the cat shook its head, hesitated briefly, and headed back for the trees! By this time the fawn was bounding for the timber on this side of the creek. Its mother changed direction and went after the cat for a few strides, but, apparently satisfied her offspring was safe, she shot back across the meadow, over the creek and into the trees with her fawn.

I returned to my pancakes with a feeling of warm relief, poured a second mug of coffee, started my first pipe of the day, went out to the trailer to get the swede saw and started cutting lengths of log to stove size. I could have fired up the chainsaw, but I didn't want to shatter the relative peace of the place with the power saw's racket. Anyway, a little exercise with a swede saw wouldn't come amiss in the bracing morning air. That plus thereafter splitting the logs should put me in fair fettle for an afternoon hunt; hopefully by then Dan would have arrived.

While I was busy sawing, my retrospective mood returned, and I cast my mind back to Schonrade, the country estate of German Baron von Wedemeyer in Pomerania, some fifty or more miles from the Stargard camp.

A group of us, all NCOs (non-commissioned officers), learned the Germans were about to send a party of twenty-five or twenty-six Canadian prisoners to do farm and field work at the estate. In case I haven't explained earlier, the Geneva Convention made it plain that, while NCO and commissioned officer prisoners could not be forced to work for the enemy, those below the rank of full corporal could and often were. In many respects, the so-called "other ranks" who were sent out to work often enjoyed the break from being behind the wire, particularly if they were out on some of the farms. Not only did they subsist on farm food, they invariably received their regular issue of weekly Red Cross parcels, though sometimes the parcels didn't always arrive weekly. In addition to being able to enjoy the extra food items from that source, chocolate and real coffee in particular, being worth their weight in gold in wartime Germany, were particularly handy for trading.

They also came in even more handily for prisoners to satisfy that most basic of natural urges, especially with German females whose husbands or boyfriends had been away at the front or who would never return. Such liaisons of course were definitely frowned upon by German officialdom. The penalty for prisoners caught in such compromising circumstances, at the very least, was a stretch in a punishment cell. For a German female it brought time in jail, if not a concentration camp, and prior to going inside, having her head shaved and being paraded through the streets of her town or village wearing a notice relating her sin for all to see. Even so, the dire consequences didn't always cool the ardour of randy POWs or sex-starved *frauleins*. In fact there was a little verse some German women used to sing:

Alles voruber, alles forbei,
mein Mann ist im Russland,
mein bett is noch frei.

121

A literal translation of this verse would be as follows:

"All is over, all is past,
my man is in Russia and
my bed is now free."

Meantime, the handful of us sergeants and corporals earlier mentioned decided a good bet for possible escape would be to get out on a work party. The Schonrade caper seemed a heaven-sent opportunity even for myself, who had made more than one attempt previously, without success! So, two fellow sergeants, as well as myself from the Royals, Pat Hallaran and Bruce McDermott; together with Jack Kimberley of the Royal Hamilton Light Infantry; a couple of Black Watch corporals from Montreal whose last names only I can recall, Monk and O'Brien; and Gib Renwick, Winnipeg Camerons, started planning.

I digress momentarily here to point out that Kimberley did manage to escape, not on the Schonrade venture, but a couple of months or so later from the Stargard camp itself. Made it back to Britain via Sweden, to be awarded a DCM (Distinguished Conduct Medal) for that effort. Renwick also collected the same decoration resulting from an action of his on the Dieppe show. He was blowing the "war horns" (bagpipes) as the first wave of his regiment landed south of Dieppe. A German bullet punctured the pipe bag (clearly a German who was also a lover of good music!). The story goes that Renwick went somewhat berserk at this sacrilege and thereafter wiped out two German machine gun emplacements and one enemy blockhouse!

We redoubtable seven had to overcome one problem before we could get out with the Schonrade work party. We had to engage in what, at that stage of hostilities, had became a standard practise known as "swapping over." That is, each of us had to find a lance corporal or private whose identity we could use while he took over ours. Incidentally this practise, at times, caused a helluva mix-up when an NCO who had already swapped over with one of another rank returned to the main camp to find the man with whom he'd initially swapped identities had been moved to another camp and he, the original, genuine NCO, was then shipped out on another work party under the ID of the fellow he was supposed to be!

It wasn't difficult to persuade seven fellows slated for the Schonrade detail to switch I.D.s with us, and a few days later we shipped out. When we arrived at the estate late at night, the squad of German troops was led by a sergeant who, among other decorations, wore the crimson and white ribbon of what their frontline fellows called the Frostbite Medal, awarded all who had served at least one winter on the Russian front. They shepherded us into a room in the basement of the main building, then a largely unused manor, on the estate. The room was no more than twelve or fifteen feet square, crowded with three-tiered bunks jammed against each other. Each bunk contained a layer of loose straw. No canvas covering in which to stuff the straw. We promptly dug in our heels and said we certainly weren't going to be housed in that one room. The Germans began to get a little snarly, telling us a couple of dozen Russian prisoners had previously worked there and seemed satisfied with the sleeping arrangement. It was the first direct contact those Germans had had with Canadian prisoners, so I, as the unofficially elected interpreter, explained that not only were we as Canadians not used to such sparse accommodation but also it was extremely unhealthy, and they [the guards] certainly didn't want their new charges to fall sick and thus not be able to work for "Führer and Fatherland."

The ploy worked. The sergeant opened up three or four other connecting basement rooms, ordered his squad to help us break down the bunks to two-tier units, and lastly opened up the kitchen on that level so that we could prepare our own meals—Red Cross foodstuffs again coming in particularly handy. After all, we further explained, the better fed we were, the more work we would perform.

The revamping project was done before any of us, guards and prisoners, turned in for the night. The next day was Sunday, a day we said we didn't work. The German contingent readily agreed. They were as anxious as we for a day of rest. The remainder of the day we spent policing up our expanded quarters and settling in. The seven of us, all Anglos, commandeered a separate room for our sleeping quarters. The remainder of the prisoner work crew, all "peasoupers" from the Fusiliere de Montreal regiment, also captured at Dieppe, set up their own quarters, although we all used the same kitchen and eating section and facilities. There was nothing inherently racist in this. That's the way the Frenchmen wanted it, and it was fine with us.

With the coming of the next day came our second ploy. I explained to the German NCO that, to maintain our living quarters in clean and healthy fashion, it would necessitate two of us staying there each day to sweep, wash floors and windows and generally keep things neat and tidy. Furthermore, we set it up so that two different fellows took on the janitorial duties every couple of days. I had already established I couldn't go out to work because, as interpreter, I'd be needed in our quarters as well as outside to pursue that job when and where instructions and orders from the Germans and requests of them from us needed translation.

Our best con job however, for which I cannot claim lone credit much as I would have liked, was a combined effort. We were actually able to persuade the Germans we had to have an added interpreter available at all times, between the French and ourselves. It worked. Finally, every day we had one fellow go sick. All in all, of a contingent of a couple of dozen prisoner workers, every day five, and sometimes when an extra man reported sick, six Canadians simply didn't do a damned thing for the other side.

Not that much was accomplished even by those who did go out supposedly to work. One of our Anglo covey one day was particularly industrious in the cowbarns. It was one of the Black Watch duo, but I cannot recall which. Somehow, from somewhere, he came into possession of some permanganate of potash crystals. These he busily, and secretly, mixed with the mash for the cattle. A day later, all the cows on the estate were pissing purple. We never did find out if the Germans discovered what was the cause of this interesting phenomenon. More to the point, they never caught up with the perpetrator.

However, the main thrust of this digression from my sawing and splitting chore that morning at Far Meadow came when Kimberley,

Renwick, Hallaran and McDermott went to work at the little schnapps factory on the estate grounds. They were in the charge of one guard and the old fellow who was the von Wedemeyer family's lifelong brewmaster, or whatever is the specific title for whoever distils that most acceptable form of libation. During the first few days of their employment, the quartet established good rapport with brewmaster and guard, largely by way of judicious distribution of cigarettes. Their specific task was to work just outside the little distillation plant, sawing lengths of timber to feed the fire of the still.

I was not aware of what was going on until I heard a shot fired. At the time I was inside the house in which the Baroness von Wedemeyer was residing, a wartime measure I gather, since the large house was no longer used by the family for parties and entertaining guests. She was a very pleasant woman. Her husband was a colonel in a Panzer regiment who had just returned to France following a leave period. She had been showing me her son's room. He had died in Russia the previous year, and among other memorabilia of him, his field cap, with a bullet hole in it, rested on a dressing table in the room. Laid before the cap were his medals and behind it a picture of him in full uniform. I remember mentally saluting him for, after all, he too had been a soldier, and we were then about the same age, in our late twenties.

The sound of the shot startled the lady and myself, and we both rushed out to find the cause. I ran ahead of her in the direction of the schnapps factory from where the shot had come. The guard was being berated by a large, beefy fellow wearing a hunting jacket, breeches and boots. He was the so-called Inspektor, a Nazi party bureaucrat assigned by the party to the estate to make sure the requisite amount of crops, meat and schnapps were being set aside for army and civilian consumption. It was the first time we'd seen him, although we knew of his presence a day or so after we arrived there. He was the epitome, to use Churchill's phrase, "The Hun [who] is either at your throat, or at your feet," a loud, boorish, bullying type who was at the moment venting his spleen on the guard.

The German sergeant reached the scene the same time as myself. He in turn began shouting at the Nazi official. The Inspektor had blasted the guard for not following his order to shoot one of the quartet of Canadians, the aforementioned Kimberley, Renwick, McDermott and Hallaran. All had been standing around smoking, the guard with them, when the Nazi thug appeared. Smoking was strictly forbidden anywhere in the immediate area of the farm buildings and schnapps factory. The bureaucrat seemingly made no impression on the four with his screaming and ranting, so he had turned his attention to the guard, ordering him to stop smoking and, if the prisoners didn't immediately stop, to shoot one of 'em. Finally the guard, more for show than anything else, fired into the air.

The guard NCO threatened to shoot the Inspektor if he didn't get his ass out of there right away. The Nazi strode off, threatening to report the whole affair to the Germans' superior officers; the sergeant gave the guard a tongue lashing (again I suspect more for show than real effect) for smoking, and peace of a sort returned. But it didn't last.

After the lunch break, Messrs. Renwick, Kimberley, Hallaran and McDermott spotted the Nazi functionary skulking along on the far side of a barn across from the schnapps plant, obviously bent on nabbing them again for smoking or some other sin. They decided to have a little more fun at his expense, and all began sawing away at logs resting on sawhorses. If I recall correctly, Kimberley and McDermott were vigorously pulling and pushing at either end of a two-man crosscut, Hallaran and Renwick working away at the other. What was so interesting to watch, however, was that all were using the saws upside down!

They would furiously saw away, making no impression whatsoever on the logs, of course. Then they'd stop, look in puzzlement at the unmarked chunks of wood, and start again, taking care once more to use the top side of the saw blade. It didn't take long for the Party poohbah to charge out from his hiding place and to once again start ranting and raving. The guard, of course, knew exactly what they were doing and why; and I will admit, difficult though it was, he kept a straight face as he patiently attempted to explain at the Nazi fellow's screamed urgings precisely how to use a crosscut saw correctly. The four in turn continued their act, looking blankly at guard and Inspektor. I wandered over, to be collared by the latter to translate what he and the guard were saying. This farce continued for all of half an hour before the Nazi stormed away, raving about idiot prisoners, especially Canadians, who were supposed to be great woodsmen but couldn't seem to grasp the elementary fact that, to saw wood, you have to use the teeth of the implement.

By the next day word of the Party man's double defeat had spread throughout the estate. Germans, military and civilian, seemed as amused as ourselves and, if anything, a contingent of Polish civilian workers even more so. Apparently, prior to our arrival on the scene, the Inspektor had made life unbearable for Poles and German civilians alike, the only person he had hitherto not been able to faze being the Baroness.

The following morning, we Canadians went through our usual morning routine of lining up, numbering off, and answering our own roll call. Just for the hell of it. Then the various work parties were marched off to their various tasks.

The Schnapps squad were all set for what they and the rest of us fervently hoped would be the final bout with the Inspektor. Sure enough, as they reached the factory, he was seen sneaking around to the back of the structure. They waited a few minutes, then broke out the cigarettes, lighted up, and took up their saws to resume the pantomime of the previous day. Meantime, the old brewmaster was peering out of a window on the second floor of the factory, looking down along the wall at the foot of which the Inspektor was slowly moving along in a crouched position. The old fellow silently signalled the quartet as to what was occurring. As the Nazi moved closer to the end of the wall, preparing, they figured, to spring out and catch them in the act again, Renwick stepped up to the front wall of the plant and waited. When the brewmaster signalled that the Inspektor was at the point where he could make his surprise entry to the scene, Gib sprang around the corner of the building and yelled, "Boo."

It scared the you-know-what out of the benighted and befuddled Inspektor, who then started screaming and raging to the point where he literally began frothing at the mouth. As he thumped his way from the area, he was still shouting to himself and waving his arms.

We didn't see him again. About two weeks later we were all shipped back to Stargard before we could get fully weaving on, let alone finalize, our escape plans. I rather believe the Poles and Germans, even our guards, were sorry to see us depart—especially Renwick, Hallaran, McDermott and Kimberley, who could, I believe, be rightly called "party poopers!"

I have often wondered how, if at all, the Baroness survived the war.

Back at Far Meadow, I was just finishing my wood cutting and stacking when I heard a vehicle a couple of miles back in the timber. Fifteen or twenty minutes later, the Jimmy appeared, the Tigger driving and waving at me. By the time he reached the cabin, I had a mug of coffee poured and had started making sandwiches ready for the afternoon hunt.

*1967 picture, Russian memorial
to thousands dead in battle for Berlin*

CHAPTER 14
AN AWFUL LOT OF BULL!

Dan and I set off mid-afternoon, headed back to the meadow where I had seen the young bull moose the previous morning. A trail runs from the cabin, along the north side of the first meadow immediately to the west, the same meadow where I'd seen the bobcat stalking the doe and dawn.

We reached the far end of a section of fence that had been taken down some time in the past when someone, possibly members of Eagle Lake Henry's band, had driven horse-drawn wagons through to haul hay from the second meadow. There the Tigger went up and back into the trees a couple of hundred yards while I continued walking just above the trail, no more than a hundred feet into the timber. We invariably walk in that fashion, keeping each other in occasional sight. In this manner, if he spooks game it most likely will move down to the meadow to cross at the narrowest point into the trees on the other side; thus, providing I had my wits about me, I may see the animal and get a chance of a clear shot unimpeded by trees or undergrowth.

By now the sun had dissipated the frost from grass and brush except for some areas still in deep shadow under the trees. Walking very slowly and quietly, stopping every few yards and starting again, it would take us all of an hour to reach the end of the second meadow where it swung south toward still another lake, fed and drained by that portion of Brittany Creek.

It was good to have the Tigger along. I think I have already made plain, of all those who have hunted with me and with whom I've hunted, he remains my best and closest friend, hunting and fishing partner. In recent years he's become less interested in shooting and more enthusiastic about fishing, but he still enjoys being way back in the high country with me even though he knows I'm not concerned should he not wish to shoot. I, of course, welcome his presence because of his expertise and experience with vehicles; also, he's much more capable nowadays of hefting and packing meat than I.

Many are those who have contributed to the backcountry and woodsy wisdom and education of my son, beginning with Alan Blackwell, from whom he learned from the start how to move quietly and with economy of effort through the timber. Those few days he spent with Blackwell many years ago when I took him up country for his seventh birthday offered basic learning he has never forgotten.

That was also the first time I heard the lad enquire solicitously, "Can I help you, da?" Blackwell was leading us through the timber on the far side of Eutsuk Lake, over much of the area he'd travelled looking for that strayed American hunter the day we were waiting for Alan in Prince George. Walking right behind Alan, almost on his heels, Dan hopped over windfalls with the agility of a mountain goat. I was some yards behind both. Every so often the boy would turn, make sure I was following, and as I clambered rather than jumped over the windfalls, he'd give forth with his question.

Another who had a profound and lasting impression on Dan is the fellow I've hitherto referred to as the Ancient Mariner, Alf Poole. Poole is more fishing than hunting oriented also, and it is from him, I believe, the Tigger came by his penchant for that pastime. No matter where he travelled in this province or the rest of Canada, even on union business, Poole always took fishing tackle, just in case. One of his proudest accomplishments in that regard, I gather, came after completing union business for the day up in the Northwest Territories. He went out to fish for, and caught, Arctic Char at midnight. From Poole, Dan learned many baiting and casting techniques, augmented in later years by what he learned from the Frenchman, Julien Patenaude.

I must point out that it was from Poole as well that the Tigger's education was greatly expanded in the use of the right expletives in the appropriate circumstances, colourful adjectives being certainly not lacking in Poole's lexicon. One of the first times I took Dan along with Poole and myself to fish the Merritt country, we were driving up the Fraser Canyon headed for Spence's Bridge and the road into Merritt from there. As many will know, on the right side of the highway near Boston Bar there is an Indian graveyard. As we passed it that day, the Tigger asked Poole if there were any famous Indians buried there.

"Certainly," came the straight-faced reply. "That's where Chief Klutch-um-Dink is buried."

It took the young'un all of a couple of minutes to get the point. However, on our return home, much to Poole's discomfort, Dan told the story to his mother while we were having dinner. Alf's discomfort wasn't eased any by the fact that this was the first time he'd met and dined in the company of my lass.

A further incident involving Poole came back to haunt Lila. It initially arose on the first hunting trip Poole made with me, and it followed my interview, mentioned in an earlier chapter, with Howard Mitchell about his battle to re-establish California Bighorn in Farwell Canyon. After leaving Mitchell's office, as we were preparing to head for his cabin at Farwell, Poole insisted he wanted to do some last minute food shopping in Williams Lake. Bear in mind, as with every up country trip I take, we already had enough victuals to last twice as long as we intended being out. But the cantankerous Ancient Mariner was undeterred, so he and the Tigger trooped into the supermarket to get a few extras, including what Poole referred to as "horse cock"—an impolite description for a variety of salami.

Weeks later, Dan was with his Mum when they were at the Woodward's food section at the Guildford Mall. She was doing her Christmas food shopping. At one point, the Tigger clearly and distinctly implored his mother to "get some horse cock"—one of those times most mothers have experienced when their immediate desire is to, just as clearly and distinctly, tell all within earshot, "He's not my kid!"

I like to think I have had a measure of input into Dan's woodsy education too, but in addition to those previously mentioned, I reckon none had a greater impact on him in this regard than the Schuks, particularly Cal and Cliff. Today he walks much more easily than I over distances anywhere up to ten miles or more through all types of backcountry; he is far more adept at handling and maintaining vehicles in the bush and, as the years go by, I believe he will gain as great a love of the wilderness as I have been fortunate to acquire.

One I would dearly have loved the Tigger to meet before he went to his reward while Dan was in his infancy was Eric Collier. However, Dan does have my copy of *Three Against the Wilderness*, Collier's priceless classic of wilderness lore, life and living. Always before me is the manner in which this late, great hunter, trapper, guide and conservationist (long before that became the buzzword of the cocktail party set, the pseudo-intellectual literati and less than pragmatic politicians) inscribed my copy of his book and which says it all so well: "In pleasant recollection of good years gone, with very best wishes for those that are left."

Dan and I, he still paralleling me back in the trees, had now reached the end of the second meadow, and we both were making the turn south. Almost directly opposite me, on the other side and under the trees, I saw the bull. I was sure it was the one I'd seen the previous day. As I watched, there was a movement behind him and, sure enough, there was a cow was with him. Both were walking slowly eastward. Suddenly from behind me and some yards to my left came a cracking sound. I knew it wasn't Dan because I'd caught a glimpse of him above and to the right of me only moments before. I couldn't see him now, but I was sure he too had heard the sound. I froze and waited. It wasn't long before the outline of the head and rack of another bull showed above an outcrop of willow at the top of a slight rise. He too was walking slowly down toward the open meadow, in the direction of the other bull.

When the bull to my left stepped into the meadow proper, I could see he was a larger and older bull than the fellow on the other side. He lifted his head and I distinctly heard his short, coughing call. It was the prelude to something I had hitherto never seen in my years of hunting and walking the backwoods. From across the meadow came another call and up behind me the sound of a number of animals moving about. The scene was set. The older bull already had a harem of cows and was calling the single cow that was with the younger bull across the meadow. The younger bull, meantime, was trying to attract the older fellow's females.

A slight sound to my right caused me to turn, and there was the Tigger. He was now fully aware of what was happening. As he stealthily joined me, both bulls charged from either side into the middle of the meadow. They met on our side of the creek with a crash that sounded like a number of trees falling. For the next ten minutes or so, their heads weaving from side to side when they backed off a few yards, then ramming heads and racks against each other's, the two bulls battled. My camera and tape recorder were miles back at the cabin. A classic, once-in-a-lifetime confrontation between two of the largest members of the deer family anywhere in the world and neither of us was able to record it on tape or film.

As abruptly as the fight had begun, it ended. The younger bull turned and ran off to the west, away from his adversary, and away from his lone cow. The old bull loped a few steps toward her, then about-faced; and, as he moved back to our side of the meadow and his harem, she followed and joined them. I now had a clear shot at the old bull about eighty yards to my left. He went down as the shell hit him in the chest. I was able to put a second shot behind his ear before he could move from where he'd fallen. The Tigger didn't need, nor for that matter wish, to fire. As I mentioned earlier, he now much prefers to fish rather than shoot big game; but he carries a rifle just in case, for which I have added respect for him. As I have also previously pointed out, he is good to have with me when the work begins, and such was now the case.

As I started opening up the old bull, Dan set off back to camp. By the time I had the chest cavity propped open with stout sticks of jackpine and had removed the innards, I heard the sound of the Jimmy motor. When it stopped, I realised that he had driven as far as he could, which was the other end of that meadow. It wasn't long before he reached on foot the place where I was working. He'd brought packboards, into which we stuffed heart and liver, and by that time dusk was fast approaching. He had also brought a couple of flashlights, but I decided we'd leave the skinning and quartering until next morning. By then the animal would be well chilled out. We took our time walking to the vehicle, and it was dark by the time we got to the cabin.

After relighting the fire and with the lamp hissing away at full bore; I mixed my olive soup while the Tigger was enjoying a pre-dinner beer. "So, Dad," he asked, "why did you shoot the old bull instead of the young one?"

"Well, first," I explained, "the old fellow was closest. Since he was on the side of the meadow where we were; we didn't have to haul him across the creek. Besides," I added, tipping my glass toward him, "since he'd obviously had a number of seasons with cows, I reckon it was time for the young bull to have a full fling." Which doubtless he was now doing, or was about to.

The discussion reminded me of the story of the old Hereford bull standing with a younger bull on a small hill looking down on a herd of healthy cows. The young bull started pawing the ground and, turning to his older companion, said, "Let's charge down there and screw one of those cows."

The old bull said, "Let's walk down, and screw 'em all!"

Next day Dan and I completed the butchering by noon. Then came the task of poling out between us the quarters, each of which weighed between 160 and 180 pounds. Judging across the close to three miles we had to heft that meat, over hummocks of grass and the odd fallen tree before we reached the trailer hitched behind the Jimmy, I swear to this day the balls of that old bull weighed twenty-five pounds apiece! Leastways that's the way they felt by the time we'd carried out the last quarter, it being one of the rules of the game that the testicles must not be removed, so as to satisfy game wardens that the animal was in fact a male.

With the quarters wrapped in cheesecloth, once we were finally back at camp, and hanging in trees just behind the cabin, we spent another night there and left the next morning. Neither of us has been back to Far Meadow since, but, "with particularly pleasant recollections of many good years gone [up in the magnificent Chilcotin], I look forward to many that are left," with good friends— and the best of these is the Tigger.

CHAPTER 15
ISRAELI ASSIGNMENT

Irony of ironies! Following my first visit to Germany in the spring of 1967 since my "enforced visit" during 1942 to '45, I was back in my home base (Vancouver) only a few days when the famed "Six Day War" of June 1967 broke out. Sooo...within days it was back overseas on assignment to cover that conflict. However, by the time I arrived in Israel the conflict was over! Let me offer my views on that experience before I discuss the earlier return to Germany as it was a learning experience that has affected the way I remember my German experiences both during and after the Second World War.

I landed in Israel on Sunday, June 11, 1967, by which time the Israelis had finished the lightning strikes they had made west across the Sinai desert as far as the Suez Canal; south to the Red Sea; east into the Golan Heights and into the Syrian town of Kuneitra. In fact, as I learned later, it was that advance that caused the panic-stricken Syrian government a few miles away in Damascus to call at the United Nations Security Council meeting in New York for an immediate cease-fire. Jordan and Egypt promptly followed suit. Had the Israelis not then accepted the cease-fire call, there is no doubt they would have advanced the few miles beyond Kuneitra to take Damascus and would have occupied that first capital city of the Arab coalition, led by then Egyptian dictator Gamel Nasser.

It is true the Israelis the week before launched what subsequently became known as a "pre-emptive strike" under the code name "Strike Zion." They had no choice. It is an axiom of life in Israel that while its Arab neighbours can retreat and invariably do when in battle against Israel, Israel cannot. Arab states can and have lost wars against Israel. Israel cannot. Should Israel lose one of these conflicts, it will be her last. The chant and policy of her immediate Arab neighbours has long been to "drive Israel into the sea." By and large, that has been the chant and policy of those Arab states for decades, long before Israel became an independent nation; long before as well, as during the Second World War, the then leading Muslim spokesman in British-occupied Palestine, the Grand Mufti, a fervent Nazi admirer, called for the extermination of Jews.

In many respects, it was fortunate that I arrived in Israel when I did because, aided by the Israeli assigned to me for my subsequent tour of the newly Israeli-conquered territories, I was able to move around accompanied only by the said Israeli, a "sabra" or Israeli-born Jew, Yitzak Sasson. This state of affairs allowed me independence from the large coterie of foreign reporters and correspondents being conducted through the newly occupied areas by officials of the Israeli Military. In these circumstances, it was possible for me to phone nightly reports to my Vancouver outlet throughout my tour without going through IMG (Israeli Military Government) censors. This was particularly helpful, via the good offices of Sasson, in that, on a number of occasions, I was able to send despatches using the signals equipment of Israeli units in the field.

* * *

ISRAELI VERBAL WANDERINGS: "Sinai and Suez"
Returning to my earlier remark apropos Israel having no choice but to launch its "pre-emptive strike" that triggered the Six Day conflict, one must cast one's mind back over a decade from then to the 1956 Suez conflict. That in turn came about as a result of Egypt's blocking of the Suez Canal, causing Britain and France to attempt a breaking of the blockade with military action supported by Israel because, in the same process, Egyptian president Nasser threatened Israel's trading outlets with his policy, since coming to power a few

years earlier, of refusing to allow Israeli ships to pass through the Suez Canal en route to ports in south and west Africa, India, the Far East and Australasia.

All the above, in turn, triggered concerns that a third world conflict might erupt, given that Russia and China were supporting Egypt in particular in the Arab anti-Israel case and cause in general. Out of this, what became known as UNEF, the United Nations Emergency Force, came into being. UNEF was the brainchild of Canada's then Foreign Secretary, Lester ("Mike") Pearson. UNEF's formation followed a United Nations, strongly American-backed, call for a Mid-East ceasefire, which in turn brought the withdrawal of the British, French and Israeli troops from the Suez-Sinai area. For his efforts in this, Pearson won a Nobel Peace Prize, and for the next decade an uneasy kind of peace reigned in the area. It was, however, a "ceasefire" in name only. Egyptian forces spasmodically fired into Israeli settlements along the Sinai and Gaza borders, while on the other side of Israel Syrian guns and tanks, hunkered down in bunkers along the eastern shores of the Sea of Galilee, fired almost daily into Israeli settlements below from the safety of the Golan Heights. Although members of the UNEF (which included some Canadian troops) were supposed to maintain peace along the earlier mentioned border areas, their presence had no impact.

Such attacks continued throughout the next decade. Then, in the spring of 1967, Nasser ordered UNEF out and without even a whimper of protest from the UN Security Council, UNEF withdrew. The Egyptian dictator Nasser had long contended that since becoming Egyptian president and despite international opinion, a state of war existed between Israel and the so-called UAR (United Arab Republics, primarily made up of Egypt, Syria, Jordan and Iraq, with Nasser as self-appointed leader). Furthermore, the avowed intention of the UAR was the destruction of the State of Israel. Thus, when Nasser succeeded in forcing the withdrawal of the UNEF in May 1967, Israel knew she faced two choices. She could continue to honour the tenuous, supposed ceasefire of 1956-57 while diplomats, thousands of miles away in New York, endlessly debated Israel's future, or she could strike before her Arab neighbours moved in on all sides to carry out their avowed intention. Thus came the "pre-emptive strike" or under its code name, "Strike Zion."

I should have seen it coming. In fact, I did see it coming but reacted slowly. I can take some sort of refuge in the fact that I was not alone. World leaders, intelligence agencies, international observers had no hint of when and how fast the Israelis moved.

In retrospective, of course, I could have been faster off the mark had I continued on from my German assignment in May '67 and jetted to Israel instead of returning to my Canadian home base. However, I repeat my earlier point that, having arrived in Israel the weekend of the ceasefire and thus taking off with my Israeli guide-translator, I was in a much better position to visit the newly occupied Israeli areas unhindered by officially guided-tour officials and censorship via those officials. And so, the Monday following the weekend ceasefire, I travelled west from the town of Jaffa into the Sinai proper.

Late in the day we arrived at Khan Yunis, a small village newly occupied by elements of an Israeli armoured unit. On reporting to an Israeli major, we asked permission to bivouac with those troops for the night. He agreed but said that we'd better double check with the colonel. In answer to our next query, he said we should find the colonel outside, back of the former Egyptian school being used as headquarters for the Israeli unit.

Behind the school were some vehicles but no Israeli troops. Then I spotted the feet of someone beneath a half-track vehicle and asked if he could tell us where to find the colonel. The rest of the body followed the feet as they came out from under the half-track. As the fellow stood up, he said, "I'm the colonel. What can I do for you?"

This was the first of many similar experiences during my tour of newly occupied areas. It was often difficult to distinguish between ranks in the various units we encountered. In fact, a general of paratroops in the '67 campaign who later became Israeli prime minister Ariel Sharon is said to have described his troops as "a mob" often "improperly dressed." The fact remains, of course, the IDF

(Israel Defence Force) is made up of some of the finest, man for man (and woman for woman), fighting troops in the world, but without the swagger of troops from countries with histories of conflict and conquest in past and present military actions.

This state of affairs surfaced that same evening when, together with Sasson, I was invited to join the colonel and two O's (other ranks) on a night patrol into the desert aboard the same half-track on which the colonel had been working when we first met earlier that day. A sergeant was in charge of the patrol. We didn't encounter any Egyptian troops that evening, although some isolated pockets of enemy units were being "mopped up" throughout the area

On returning from the patrol and before turning in for the night, we sat around in the school chatting and drinking orange juice. I noticed the Israelis observed me rather closely as I looked around the room. What took my attention were a couple of small maps of the eastern Mediterranean in the schoolroom. It took me a few minutes to realise that both maps, which had been printed in Cairo, presented Egypt from the Sinai running east to the Jordanian border, Jordan all the way west to the Mediterranean and from the north, Syria extending to the Egyptian and Jordanian territory. Finally it struck me—Israel was not shown on either map. Its territory was subsumed by the members countries of the UAR! Egyptian and equally obviously Syrian and Jordanian children were taught Israel simply didn't exist—a contention that would seem to remain to the present time in the minds of many Arabs, some of whom are the makers of Arab policies even now, especially among such as Yasser Arafat and many of his supporters throughout much of the present-day Middle East.

The day following my night patrol and "map revelations," Sasson and I journeyed west along the Sinai coast road to El Arish, a beautiful oasis with magnificent palm trees, which was occupied by a paratroop unit. I was allowed to take pictures of part of the oasis but not any of the military equipment therein, which included sophisticated radar equipment. Another Israeli senior officer did tell me, however, that the third day of the Sinai campaign when they overran El Arish, the Israelis used the Egyptian radar and Arabic speaking Israelis to "talk down" half a dozen Russian MIG fighter aircraft sent from Libya to help their Egyptian allies. The Libyans were obviously "conned" into believing the propaganda pouring out of Egypt, Syria and Jordan that the Israelis were being destroyed on all fronts. Thus, at El Arish, the MIG's were quickly and quietly captured, intact, by the Israelis, and their pilots taken prisoner. I subsequently learned those jet fighters were the latest Russian models, which had not yet seen service with the Russian air force. Indeed, it was not until many months later that, having thoroughly examined the planes themselves, the Israelis would allow American and British military officials to examine them.

One of the main segments of the Israeli pre-emptive strike involved their air force hitting Egyptian, Jordanian and Syrian airfields during the first day of the war, with the result that few Arab planes even managed to take off. The Israelis never countered spurious Arab claims of massive air victories. Thus the self-deception worked to Israel's advantage, as the El Arish ploy clearly showed. Similarly, in the Sinai campaign, Israeli armoured units were able to cut off and surround Egyptian and Syrian units, often before the latter were able to fire a shot. As in Jordan and Syria, much if not most of the tanks the UAR employed were Russian; and again it is claimed that, like the El Arish jets, this was even before the Russians ever saw these latest model tanks perform. There was a story, probably apocryphal, that mid-week in the Sinai fighting Nasser telephoned Soviet president Alexei Kosygin requesting more tanks. Kosygin is reputed to have replied, "Certainly, how many does Dayan [Israeli Defence Minister Moshe Dayan] want?"

The Israeli armoured units were equipped with vintage Second World War American Shermans and British Centurions in the main. They faced upward of eighty-thousand Egyptian infantry—five infantry divisions—and over nine hundred tanks, mostly Russian T-54's. Even as their air force moved initially against Arab airfields in Egypt, Libya, Jordan and Syria, the Israeli armoured units drove west towards the Suez, in the process coming up behind Egyptian units. I later learned that Defence Minister Dayan, Chief of the Israeli General Staff Yitzhak Rabin and his Deputy Chief Chaim Balev possessed some archaeological knowledge. Thus, they knew of old Roman roads traversing areas of the Sinai just below the desert surface, which meant that their armour was invariably able to move against enemy units and installations without becoming bogged down in the sand! On our trek west, Sasson and I saw literally hundreds of captured Egyptian tanks, which had sustained little or no damage in the Israeli dash for the Suez Canal.

Once we reached the canal, one of the first things Sasson wished to do, having never before seen the waterway, was to have me take a picture of him sitting there. At that juncture also I was to once again make use of Israeli signals equipment to phone direct reports to my home base to report, among other items, the fact that the Egyptian Red Crescent, the Arab equivalent of the Red Cross, was plying across the Canal from the Egyptian western bank of the waterway to ferry Egyptian prisoners back home. In this fashion I was able to correct earlier claims put out by Egyptian reports that the Israelis were not allowing the Red Crescent to operate in this fashion and that they were not allowing Egyptian prisoners to be repatriated. As one Israeli officer told me, "We simply can't afford to feed and water these people."

Another story I heard while at the Suez was that the Israelis would have moved across the Canal before the ceasefire came into effect if not, at the time, Dayan had been facing north when he reached the waterway. Because of his subsequently internationally recognized eye-patch, which covered his blind eye, he simply didn't see the other side of the Canal in time to move his troops across before the ceasefire!

After spending the night with the Israeli units in El Quantara, we took off early next morning heading southeast, back across the Sinai to the former Jordanian border, thence north to spend the night in Beersheba. It was at that point that my tape recorder refused to operate. My supply of backup batteries was of no help. Beyond that, I was of no help either. Indeed, as any who have had the good fortune (or otherwise!) to know me over the years, especially those in the "electronic media" can readily attest that, when it comes to things mechanical and/or electronic, I will admit to being "technically challenged"! Although I in the past have been known to replace a ribbon in my high tech Olivetti typewriter successfully without getting too many bruises, I still by far feel more comfortable with my trusted notepad and pencil, and I am justifiably proud of my honed ability to repair (sharpen) said instrument! However, Sasson, as proved out on more than one occasion, came up with a solution. It chanced he had a cousin who, having just returned from his stint with his Israeli Defence unit and their duties in the desert, was once more ensconced in his radio and electronic repair shop in Beersheba. After he'd cleaned out the Sinai sand in the tape machine, my problem was solved.

That evening in the hotel dining room, Sasson and I were the only customers, but we enjoyed a pleasant meal. Since the small bar was open in our honour, a lone, very attractive belly dancer from Algeria first performed for us then asked to be allowed to join us for a post-dinner drink. Once it was established that I wasn't prepared to buy her champagne cocktails, she settled for a glass or two of sweet vermouth. Between sips, in an intriguing mix of Hebrew-Arabic-French and English punctuated with many "damns," "hells" and the occasional well pronounced "fucks," we heard how she hoped eventually to become an international dance performer. The evening ended with her going her way and Sasson and myself retiring, having been greatly entertained by her admittedly delightful dance and a multi-lingual story that I also have to admit was well worth the cost of the drinks!

We spent a couple of days in Beersheba, during which time Sasson made contact with more relatives (seems he had them in almost every place we visited), a point, incidentally that, again, proved helpful to us later in our tour. Meantime, while Sasson was meeting his familial obligations, I was updating my impressions of our tour thus far for a report I had promised to make to our then Canadian Prime Minister, Lester (Mike) Pearson, following my post-Six Day War Israeli visit. It was also while we were in Beersheba that I began to assess some of the Biblical history of my first visit to the "Holy Land" and environs. For example, the Biblical name for Beersheba had been Be'er Sheva, where servants of the patriarch Isaac are said to have dug a well that, to the present, still supplies water to that area. Also during this time of "updating" I learned that the city of Gaza was the site of Samson's destruction of a temple, which followed his being blinded by the Philistines. The name Gaza is said to be the origin of the word "gauze" and was derived from a textile manufactured in Gaza during Biblical times.

On leaving Beersheba we headed north towards Jerusalem. A few miles out of Beersheba we crossed into newly Israeli-occupied territory that, little more than a week previously, had been held by Jordanian units of the crack Arab Legion formed some years earlier by an English officer, John Glubb, better known later as Glubb Pasha. Within hours of Israel's pre-emptive strike, these Arab Legionnaires, whose units and bases were destroyed by Israeli jet fighter-bombers, were forced to surrender as Israel moved to straighten out the bulge of Jordanian territory west of the Jordan River and the Dead Sea. As they fought their way through that territory, Israeli ground troops were engaged in bitter firefights with Legion Troops, often having to use infantry weapons against Jordanian armour. The Legionnaires sited tanks against the walls of such as the church of the Nativity in Bethlehem. The Israelis suffered their highest and most severe casualties in those battles. They were ordered not to use heavy artillery or airborne bombing raid against such targets because they did not wish to destroy those ancient holy places in the process.

While Sasson and I were en route to Jerusalem as night fell our vehicle, a small passenger car, began to experience engine problem. Once again, my being "mechanically challenged" meant that I was of no help. However, Sasson, being more adept at such things, soon realised we had "grounded out" on some of the rocks on the barely discernible road towards our next target, a former Arab Legion headquarter a couple of miles or so away. We could see the light of the place but, rather than abandon the vehicle, we used the undulating road surface to push the car up a slope, then have it roll down to the other side and, in some sections, gain enough momentum to carry it over the next hump. Not the most pleasant of tasks. It was a hot night, and it also struck us that, knowing small groups of un-surrendered Arab troops were said to be active in this former Jordanian territory, we weren't exactly equipped to fight off any surprise attack. Sasson's armament consisted of one Webley .32 calibre British pistol, while I carried only a camera and tape recorder. Had we encountered an Arab force of any size we might well have had more to worry about than a "sick" motor vehicle!

Fortunately, we reached the outpost, now occupied by elements of an Israeli paratroop regiment, without incident. Once again, a Sasson family connection was on hand. Specifically, the senior transport NCO of the Israeli unit turned out to be still another cousin. When Sasson and his latest cousin descended into the pit to examine the underside of our vehicle, Sasson showed more concern than did the cousin, who pronounced the damage to be repairable if we were willing to spend a day or more with those troops. While Sasson was in the pit with his cousin as he looked over the damage, he kept using an expletive he'd obviously picked up from me during our tour thus far ..."Jesus Christ"... a remark that caused the duty officer observing the mechanical check-up with me to observe, "He's not going to help YOU!" The officer, in his civilian pursuit, was a Rabbinical student.

During the next couple of days, I was privileged to go out on patrol with elements of the paratroop unit. While fraternizing with these fellows, I was struck by the fact that, whenever I went among Israeli soldiers, I was initially accepted with the traditional Jewish greeting,."Shalom" [Peace], and thereafter many times heard the same remark—not "Look what we did" (in battle) but the question: "Why did we have to do it?" I took this as another example, it would seem, of the general Israeli sentiment, even though for months prior to the Six Day War and continuous UAR belligerence and promises to "drive Israel into the sea," culminating in Nasser's forcing the UN force from the Gaza Strip; still the UN Security Council discussed and debated; in effect, the Security Council "fiddled" while the UAR planned the "burning" of the less than 20-year- old State of Israel. Israel's then ambassador to the UN, Abba Eban, put it most succinctly: "We were obliged to move from serious danger to successful resistance."

On arriving in Jerusalem a few days later, since that was his hometown, Sasson went to visit his wife and immediate family, while I spent a few days of what might be called "recuperative R&R" at the King David Hotel. During that time, Sasson also established contact with a Christian Arab friend whom he hadn't seen since boyhood. They had been separated by the partitioning of the Holy Land by international decree in the late forties, following termination of the former British mandate. The internationally imposed boundaries of that era split in two the city of Jerusalem, ceding the major eastern segment of the city to Jordan. This included the Wailing Wall, the remaining segment of Solomon's Temple, which had otherwise been destroyed by the Romans. Sasson, like many of his age group, had never been allowed to visit the Wall while it was within the Jordanian-held section of Jerusalem. In the following days, while I did not visit the Wall, I did tour much of the rest of the Old City.

Also in Sasson's company, I met his boyhood Christian Arab friend and his family and was privileged to take tea with them. The Arab, now like Sasson in his forties, was a carpenter, and I was further privileged the next day to visit his carpenter shop, the first foreign visitor so to do since before the just-ended war. A most intriguing aspect of that visit was the realisation that the Arab carpenter worked only on and with olive wood. This was particular noteworthy because the olive trees from which the wood was used were said to have been growing almost two thousand years previously, while another carpenter named Jesus of Nazareth walked, worked and preached in that part of the world! I wished to purchase some items of the Christian Arab carpenter's work, but only after I had chosen these items did he explain, via Sasson's

Arabic translation skills, that to offer payment would constitute an insult because I was being feted as the first post-war foreign visitor to the establishment. Those beautifully carved items still occupy a place in my home.

Some days later, once more accompanied by Sasson together with his boyhood pal, we were guests once more for tea, in the new Jericho home of relatives of the carpenter of Jerusalem. While there, we also visited the old, long ago abandoned Jericho, the site of another long-held Biblical legend, in which Joshua's trumpets are said to have brought down the walls.

The day following our Jericho visit, Sasson and I bade "Shalom" and goodbye to his old friend and family and headed for Khirbat Kumran by the shore of the Dead Sea, where the scrolls now given that title were found. Said to be the lowest lake in the world at more than one thousand feet below sea level, the Dead Sea is also believed to be the original Salt Sea, the waters of which are naturally, because of their salt content, completely buoyant. The air temperature in that forbidding landscape can perhaps best be described as "hotter than the hubs of hell." We did not linger long there but returned to Jerusalem for one more night of rest, ridding ourselves of deposits of sand in clothing, footwear, but remarkably not recording equipment, and made preparations for the next leg of my tour to the Sea of Galilee; the Golan Heights and the road to Damascus.

The town of Tiberias sits on the western shore at about the mid-point of the roughly fifteen-mile length of the Sea of Galilee. Across to the eastern shore, a distance of less than three miles, lie the Golan Heights, a range of hills at some points about a thousand feet high. The northernmost point of the Heights begins at the juxtaposition of the Syrian and Lebanese borders. For about forty miles, the Heights command territory due south, paralleling the Jordan River from its source in the hills close by the earlier-mentioned Syrian-Lebanese Junction. The place where the Jordan rises is known as the Baniyas. It was there, as we were to learn a few days later in conversation with Israeli paratroops, that they claimed they had uncovered a Syrian plan to poison the waters of the Jordan. Had the plan succeeded, it could have had a devastating effect downstream, since the waters of the Jordan flow into the Galilee and, further, supply Israel with its main source of fresh water. Interestingly, and remembering that I'd often heard the river referred to as "the mighty Jordan," the waterway is but a few feet wide at any given point! The river continues from the southern end of the Galilee and finishes its journey in the Dead Sea.

My Israeli guide-translator and I arrived in Tiberias on a pleasant evening to be informed by the couple who owned and operated the beautifully appointed hotel on the Galilee shore that, not only were we the only guests in the establishment but we would also enjoy the first night of absolute peace in the area in almost twenty years. Until a few days ago, when Israeli troops captured the Golan Heights, Israeli settlements below the Heights had been under spasmodic shell and gunfire. The very next day, I was able to ascertain how and why that was.

As Sasson and I toured the now Israeli-occupied Golan Heights during the next few days, I discovered that, about every half mile of the roughly forty-mile stretch of the Heights from the northern tip to the southern extremity of the Galilee, the Syrians had constructed bunkers housing heavy guns and Russian tanks, hull down sighting into and over Israeli territory below. While I was wandering through these emplacements I, at one point, heard a somewhat heated discussion some distance away between Sasson and an Israeli paratrooper major. Later I learned that the major had upbraided my guide-translator for allowing me to tour unescorted, much less unguided, into and around the bunkers. Reason for the major's concern? The area had not yet been thoroughly checked out for mines! That day ended with the pair of us beating a judiciously quick retreat back to Tiberias for the night.

The next day we were back in the Heights via the de-mined, safer road to Damascus. However, we never reached the Syrian capital. The Syrians, faced with the strong possibility that Israelis were headed for Damascus unopposed by fleeing Syrian troops, cried "Uncle" by calling plaintively for a UN monitored ceasefire. The sudden realisation that Israeli troops were within sight of two Arab capital cities, Amman in King Hussein's Jordan and Damascus in Syria and across the Suez from Egypt proper, once again gave the lie to the Arab league's own propagandistic claims of massive Arab ground troop victories and destruction of Israel's air power.

Biblical history also tells us that Saul was converted to Christianity on the road to Damascus. "Saul, Saul why persecutest thou me? It is hard for thee to 'kick against the pricks'" (Acts 26-14-15), Jesus is reported to have spoken to Saul at that time. The latter phrase of Christ's admonition has always piqued my, some would claim, irrelevant sense of humour. However, I've long believed it to be a phrase that aptly describes how taxpayers and ordinary citizens may react to the policies and pronouncements of those who govern us!

No holy admonition caused Sasson and myself to halt on the road to Damascus. Rather it was the fact that, on their drive to the Syrian capital, the Israelis halted at the town of El Khuneitra, the last Syrian outpost they reached before the hastily called ceasefire came into being, ending the Six Day War. In the years since that time, there have been numerous calls by Arab governments, and indeed even some individual Israelis, for Israel to abandon her occupation of the Golan Heights. My own opinion as a non-Jewish outsider has long been that Israel should never abandon the Heights until and unless there comes about a complete change of heart and policies by the majority of Arab leaders, which does not seem to be the case even unto the present.

Sasson and I returned to Tiberias from Khuneitra for another night before returning to Jerusalem the following day—my last day and night in the Holy Land. That last evening I was extended another courtesy when asked to dine with a senior Israel officer, who shall remain nameless for the simple reason that I was to discover he had been fully aware of my use, with Sasson's help, of Israeli signals equipment to send my various reports from newly occupied areas throughout my tour. Obviously this general officer was not averse to my dispatches, or they would never have gone through unhindered and uncensored! It was a most convivial evening, during which the host gave me much background on Israeli tactics, with the proviso that no named source could be attached to the information—a trust I have maintained to the present.

There were some half dozen other guests at dinner that evening, including a tall, dark-haired, dark-skinned Jewish woman from Yemen. She was seated next to me, and during the meal she most politely, in heavily accented English, enquired about my trip, how I reacted to what I'd seen and experienced in the occupied areas. Her questions were short, and it occurred to me that perhaps her command of English was somewhat limited but that, due to my obvious lack of Hebrew, she was attempting to play the role of convivial dinner partner. At one juncture I remarked that I was leaving the country the next day and, en route to Canada, would spend a few days in Paris, a city I had not visited at length since WWII. The young woman then asked whether I had ever heard the story of an Israeli businessman on a recent trip to the French capital. When I said not, she promptly recounted her story. The fact that the young woman continued with her story contrary to her earlier short questions quickly proved she was at ease with English, so I will try to offer her version as accurately as I remember.

"The businessman landed in Paris on a Saturday morning," she began, "and after registering at a hotel, deposited his luggage in his suite, went down to the hotel bar, made contact with one of the well-coiffed and gowned female customers in the bar and arranged to meet her that evening. Then he left to make his first business calls. Later, he indeed took the young woman out to dinner, thence to a number of nightclubs for dancing and drinks, and much later returned with her to his hotel suite."

"There," as the lady telling the story aptly described it, "they had a very active evening in bed. At the end of the boudoir gymnastics, the businessman gave the woman two hundred dollars in cash and reserved her services for the next evening, which would of course be Sunday. Later in the evening, he again picked her up as promised for another evening of wining, dining, dancing, and later yet some more active lovemaking. Following this session, he once again gave his young 'flower of the night' two hundred dollars more in cash.

"At that point," our charming storyteller informed us, "his female companion felt perhaps a mere 'Thank you' would not be sufficient in view of such largess. So she told him instead: 'This has been most enjoyable weekend. You obviously know Paris well. You certainly are familiar with the best of clubs and restaurants, you also are a connoisseur of good wine, you dance well and you make love extremely well. However," she admonished him, "you have spent an awful lot of money, including the cash you have given me. You must be a rich American tourist?'

"To this the businessman replied, 'No. Actually I'm from Tel Aviv in Israel.'

"'Really!' said the young woman. 'So am I!'

"The man smiled and remarked, 'I know. I met your mother at the airport in Israel yesterday morning as I was leaving, and she said, "If you happen to see my daughter in Paris would you be good enough to give her this four hundred dollars for me?"'"

* * *

At the outset of this segment of my "verbal meanderings," my immediate post-Six Day War assignment, I wrote, "Irony of ironies" I should explain here that the irony to which I referred lay in the fact that, within days of my German visit, I was in Israel, where many of those who fought and died as well as Israeli survivors of the June '67 battles were either survivors of, or descendents of, those who perished in the Holocaust, that Nazi abomination of the deliberately planned degradation and mass torture and murder of Jewish men, women and children, together with the wholesale deportation from their homes and homeland of Gypsies, Slavs and the mentally ill—and eventually others who also did not slavishly subscribe to the twisted Hitlerian philosophy inside Germany and all lands overrun and occupied by Germany during World War Two. All of this led ultimately to the ignominious but necessary defeat of German arms and the destruction of much of a German state that until those times had given the world a priceless legacy of music, art, architecture and culture.

Pogroms, the planned massacre and destruction of Jewish homes and holdings, began in Central and Eastern Europe and the vast Russian lands during the time of the Czars and continued under the Stalinist dictatorship. Indeed, it was not until the coming into Russian power of Gorbachev that the pogroms came to an end, although to this day it is still difficult for Jews from that part of the world to leave for life in Israel. Even so, nothing in anti-Jewish policies and programmes throughout history matched the coldly calculated Nazi "final solution." It is therefore not surprising that Nasser and Syrian leaders in particular welcomed rabid Nazis and Russian pogromists into those Arab states once the State of Israel came into being in 1948. The driving force behind that United Nations vote was the man I've long considered to have been the greatest post-Second World War American President, Harry S. Truman.

The creation of the State of Israel, however, unleashed a bitter anti-Jewish fury in most Arab states in the Middle and Near East in particular. Much of that fury and rhetoric continues into the present, epitomized by suicide bombings inside Israel and against embassies, facilities and personnel employed by governments sympathetic to the Israeli case, and at least some of this ongoing enmity seems to have been financed by Arab governments and organizations. One exception is the present King of Jordan, who favours and works toward peaceful solutions to the problem still besetting the Middle and Near East.

It is also a fact that Israel, and in particular Jerusalem, continues to house and allow to worship in their own fashion adherents to the three great religions, Jewish, Christian and Moslem, particularly involving Druze Arabs. It is also an inescapable fact that, where Israeli borders are found, the desert literally blooms. Arab states immediately surrounding Israel could do the same. Instead, they have spent literally billions on armaments, weapons of mass destruction, chemical and biological weapons and terrorist squads.

Israel remains the only parliamentary democracy in the Middle East. I have often thought of it as the keystone in that geographical arch. If ever that keystone is dislodged, the whole structure will collapse. If ever Israel loses its continuing war with its more immediate bellicose and belligerent Arab neighbours, it will indeed be Israel's "last war" and the world will be the worse for it. Throughout its existence the now little more than a half-century old independent state, Israel, has been and continues to be the world's foremost warrior against terrorism, particularly since the Black Day and date, Sept. 11, 2001, when the U.S. of A fully took up the anti-terrorism battle.

The United Nations, via its dithering following Gamel Nasser's actions against the UNEF in the spring of 1967, all but sealed the fate of the State of Israel—particularly so had the Israelis waited for the UN to act to prevent the UAR, led by Nasser, to attack Israel. Fortunately, Israeli intelligence alerted them to this and brought about her, literally, life saving pre-emptive strike. In the years since, time and again, the UN penchant to "jaw-jaw" has led many times to "war-war" with the resultant slaughter of millions of people, primarily the elderly as well as women and children, in the Balkans, parts of Africa, Asia and some Latin American countries. That situation remains extant, one of the main reasons why the United States has had to take actions in such situations as has come about involving Sadaam Hussein's Iraq.

As Churchill once pointed out, "the history of mankind is war, interrupted by brief periods of peace." I have also long believed that "a strong right arm maintains the peace." In today's world, what might well be called *pax Americana* is that "strong right arm"— certainly in the battle against international terrorism, a battle that Israel has been fighting since it was born.

Sinai desert 91km to Suez Canal right after June 67 war
Egyptian boots & helmet, foreground

Russian-made Syrian tank,
Golan Heights 1967 overlooking Israeli area

CHAPTER 16
A FINAL RETROSPECTIVE

I have been extremely fortunate in my life and times.

I count myself very much so in that I was born in this country but had the added good fortune to have spent my early years in other countries far from these shores, countries with vastly different cultures and heritages. Thus, my education in (to repeat an earlier point, that made by Lord Baden Powell decades ago) the "Varsity of Life" has been wide and eclectic, for which I can only thank my parents retrospectively.

Although my early years were spent in the relatively protected environment of British army cantonments and garrisons in the Far East, Burma briefly and a longer period in India prior to being sent to school in Britain, I did see in those early years something of the dying days of what was known as the British Raj and the Last Days of Empire. Of course I was much too young to understand much less fully appreciate what that all meant at the time. Such understanding and appreciation did not begin to materialize until, by force of circumstances beyond my control, I subsequently had to go to work for a living. One such circumstance, in all honesty, was well within my control; but, in present-day vernacular, I blew it. I failed, miserably, my university entrance exams. That turned out to have been a fortunate turn of events indeed. It enabled me to get out and about in the world on my own, away from what could have been for me the stultifying cloistered atmosphere of the halls of higher academe.

I entered into the real, outside world when much of the world, including Canada, was deep in crippling economic depression. It was a depression that hit hard and hurt most those least able to afford it and who were in no way responsible, people in middle and lower income groups. Stories of those times to the contrary, there were actually very few captains of industry and commerce who jumped to their deaths from their office towers in the canyons of financial power such as New York's Wall Street. Further, it is well nigh impossible to find records of similar suicidal deaths among the wealthy in Britain—not that there were buildings in English financial centres as tall as those of New York from which to take a final flying leap. Those who manipulated and controlled the economic strings of the then two most financially powerful nations in the world, Britain and the U.S. of A, still largely retained those manipulative powers and lost none of the creature comforts to which they had long been accustomed.

Kings and emperors were indeed gone from their palaces and powers in Russia and Germany, but others of such exalted rank and station remained very much entrenched in their privileged positions in Britain, Spain, the Scandinavian nations, in the Balkans and eastern European countries such as Romania, Yugoslavia, Greece and Albania. Even in Italy, home of the richest and most powerful of Christian orders, Roman Catholicism, and birthplace of modern Fascism, Benito Mussolini maintained the Church and the Royal House in their traditional positions of privilege and power. In countries where a semblance of democracy rather than monarchy was ascendant, France, Poland and Czechoslovakia as examples, the landed aristocratic gentry were still much in evidence if not also in government.

Even in Germany, where was spawned the most vicious and virulent form of Fascism in history, although the Kaiser had been forced into exile, it was not a particularly onerous, and certainly not pecuniary, exile. Branches of his family, courtiers and hangers-on as well as most of the large landholding privileged class, civilian and military, experienced little of the economic impact that devastated the middle and working classes of Germany during the immediate post-First-War years.

Ironically, that was also the period when Germany for the first time in its history was experimenting with the beginnings of a democratic system. Unfortunately for the Germany of that time as well as the rest of the world in future decades, the Weimar Republic lasted not much longer than Russia's only similar experiment under Keresenky.

I cite these instances to illustrate, in general fashion, the overall background for the prelude to what many still consider the last necessary big war, World War Two. It was during this time I had the good fortune to enter the world and profession of journalism, in the process gaining a priceless experience in the affairs of nations and men at a time when events were at their most volatile—indeed, from a fledgling journalist's viewpoint, also their most exciting and never to be repeated—level.

While it is fair to say that the Fascism that led inevitably to the outbreak of WWII as well as the rehearsal for it in Spain could not have survived its infancy without the active aid and comfort of the Church, the military and landed aristocracy in Italy and more so Germany; it is equally fair to say those movements could have been smothered at birth had it not been for the tacit approval, even encouragement, from many in positions of power and prominence in Britain, France and indeed the United States.

It was a time when, as very much a neophyte in the heady realm of recording world happenings and their causes, I was fortunate, metaphorically speaking, to sit at the feet of some great recorders of affairs, such as Bob Parker of Associated Press who, because of his American citizenship, was able to ride with the German armies into Poland, the Low Countries and France before the U.S. became embroiled in the war.

It was also the time that some of those still cloistered within, or who had recently graduated from, those insulating halls of higher academia at the two historically great English universities began their sometimes active, sometimes overt, sometimes deeply covert political prostitution.

To my way of thinking, it still has not been satisfactorily explained why and how it came to pass that some of the more prominent of these from Cambridge turned to deep Soviet espionage—Philby, Burgess, Maclean and Blunt—while others swung to embrace Fascism in such conclaves as what was known as the Oxford Group and the so-called Cliveden Set. An English Knight of those days, Sir Oswald Mosley became one of the more publicized darlings of many of those and other members of English high society. He led a Fascist gang, the Blackshirts—a name adopted from Mussolini's mob of thugs, who affected the same style of dress. Mosley also copied the Duce's outstretched arm salute, which became world-recognised when Hitler stole it.

It should be remembered that Mosley's mob were left free to pursue their philosophy at public rallies and in the British press of that time, including the once influential maker and breaker of governments, *The Times*. Concurrently, the traditional communist publication *Daily Worker*, though tolerated, was if anything considered the more dangerous by some press barons and the "smart set." In fact, it was considered a crime in the British army of the time, if not also the Navy and Air Force, to subscribe to that paper.

British army brass hats would have been wise in those days to have read, marked, inwardly digested and learned from Hitler's *Mein Kampf,* if for no other reason than to realise he meant what he wrote in that dull but prophetic tome. One such salient point he offered was that one of the major mistakes the German general staff of the First War was to become involved in a two-front conflict in Europe—an error, he stated, that he did not intend to make. Ultimately, of course, he was forced into that situation, which led inevitably to the defeat of his armies. In the thirties and the early days of the Second War that he launched, he successfully avoided the error by making his pact with Stalin. That allowed him to overrun Poland and the Russian dictator to assume unchallenged control of the Baltic states, a state of affairs that has only recently been publicized in Russia under Gorbachev's *glasnost*. Stalin had no illusions about the fact he would one day have to face Hitler's armies, so the Soviet dictator had to hedge his bets for the time being—more so because he had just ended a purge of his own army, having murdered more than thirty thousand of the officer corps following a series of show trials that, incidentally, were prosecuted by the man who was to become Russia's first United Nations ambassador, Andrei Vishinsky.

The early and mid-thirties witnessed Fascism on the march. Mussolini invaded and brutally subjugated Ethiopia, then known as Abyssinia. Then there was the dress rehearsal for the Second World War, the Spanish conflict. In Spain, German and Italian "advisers" to Francisco Franco's Fascists, the Falangists, helped defeat the Spanish attempt at democracy in its infancy. German and Italian military equipment and the Condor Legion composed of German Air Force pilots and planes were used in that war and brought, among other atrocities that the rest of Europe came subsequently to experience, the first indiscriminate bombings of open cities.

As much involved in the Spanish Civil War as the Fascists were communist forces. Soviet military equipment, personnel and commissars went there to aid the Republican case and cause. What Spanish Republicans didn't realise was that the Soviets wanted to turn that cause into a Russian-dominated and controlled revolution, an attempt to gain a solid foothold in western Europe. In some respects fortunately, in others not so, the Soviet ambition failed. Fortunate, that is, for the Spanish people as a whole, but unfortunate in that the Fascist win brought to Spain as repressive a regime as would have been the case had the Soviet plan succeeded. At the same time, however, repressive though it turned out to be for many Spaniards, the Franco victory ultimately assured the western powers in the upcoming world war that they could count on the Spanish peninsula as an area where escaping war prisoners as well as spies and counterspies from both side could feel fairly free to pursue their aims. It also guaranteed the British continued control of their base at Gibraltar. Meantime, if German and to lesser extent Italian participants in that war were brutal in the extreme in their treatment of Republican soldiers and Spanish civilians generally, Russian participants and many of their Spanish Republican allies were no less brutal toward Franco troops and civilian supporters.

Much of that, I suppose, comes under the heading of excesses in war. What can never be satisfactorily explained away, much less condoned, was the attitude and reaction to those excesses on the part of Franco and his troops and supporters by the two main supposed pillars of the Christian faith in Britain. In some measure the Catholic church's attitude is understandable, but not to be condoned, because of the connection between Fascism in Italy and that Church and because Franco was Catholic. The policies and pronouncements of the Church of England, however, bearing in mind its status as Defender of the Faith, still leave much to be answered for.

One of the senior *London Times* correspondents of that era whom I knew, Douglas Reed, quit that influential publication because, despite his being the paper's senior and most experienced European correspondent in the field, the publication's powers-that-be would not print his despatches detailing the war preparations of Hitler and Mussolini. Reed subsequently wrote, amoung others, four incisive and profoundly prophetic books, *Insanity Fair* (1938), *Disgrace Abounding* (1939), *Nemesis? the story of Otto Strasser* (1940) and *Prophet at Home* (1941). In the latter he stated,

Some foremost leaders of both Churches who were later loudly to call on Christians to fight 'the forces of evil' just as loudly applauded what those same forces of evil did in Spain. The sufferings of poor people there meant nothing to them. The same archbishops and cardinals who, when the bombs fell on London, were to hope they would never live through such a night as the last and who were to withdraw thereafter to the safety of the countryside, perceived quite clearly that the General whom Hitler and Mussolini were aiding in another country with bombs, tanks and men, Franco, was 'a gallant Christian gentleman'. They little cared what the forces of evil did to the fisherfolk of Almeria or the peasants of Guernica. 'Red Russia' was a 'Godless country'; Herr Adolf Hitler after all, by gad, only wished to save us from Bolshevism; Signor Mussolini 'threatened neither the religious freedom nor the security of other peoples.' The Church of England in those between war years was but the complacent Sunday-continuation-school of the (British) Tory party. If it could, it would have canonized Mr. Neville Chamberlain.

In the writing of this book, as the reader may soon realise from the outset, I have related items and incidents in a very reflective mood. I suppose this comes with age when, among other things, one has much to look back on and perhaps not that much, certainly not as many years, to look forward to. Being way back in the timber on many occasions in recent years, with rare exception being accompanied by my son, I'm inclined to look ahead to what may be his future, as well as that of his sister and others of their generation.

I dwell more specifically on the Tigger's future, his brief past, his present and what the future may hold for him than on his sister simply because he and I in his formative years have spent more time together. That is the way of it. Andrea in recent years has become interested in the outdoors in greater measure than previously, but she tends toward a more structured system of such enjoyment, much preferring the amenities afforded in national and provincial parks and campsites. Dan, like myself, prefers more the wild outdoors.

When I was Dan's age on my beginning the recording of these reminiscences, I was in a German prison camp. A few short years prior to that I was, I say again, starting to cut my teeth in journalism at a time when world and European events were moving inexorably toward the most devastating war and the greatest loss of life in recorded human history. Earlier I mentioned that many considered it the last necessary big war. So too did I, when it did come. But in the mid-thirties, along with some others, I hoped and on the whole fervently believed that it could be avoided by not surrendering principles and initiatives for its prevention to the aforementioned forces of evil.

In the fall of 1935, the leader of Italy's forces of evil, Mussolini, launched his invasion of Abyssinia. For some weeks prior, Anthony Eden, then the British Tory government's Minister for League of Nations affairs, had been pressing League members to institute sanctions against Italy should she in fact invade Abyssinia. When the Italian dictator did make his move, the Assembly of the League voted overwhelmingly to apply sanctions. But that was a paper ploy only. As soon as the vote had been taken, a committee was set up to "make further efforts for a peaceful solution." It has rightly been said that committees make much use of minutes but waste hours! This was never truer than at that time. While the League committee argued over paragraphs rather than principles, shillied over dotting "i's" and shallied over crossing "t's," Benito's brigades of brigands strafed and bombed, and gassed, thousands of Abyssinians.

Britain, having led a majority of League nations to vote for sanctions largely through the efforts of Eden, dithered under the leadership of Prime Minister Stanley Baldwin. He was aided and supported in his ditherings by the French foreign Minister, Pierre Laval—the same infamous Laval who less than half a dozen years later made the deal with Hitler to divide then conquered France, one segment being fully occupied by the Germans, the second becoming a sort of Nazi-dominated protectorate known as Vichy France.

Returning to the Italian-Abyssinian affair, Baldwin contended that sanctions could bring war with Italy and he wanted no part of that. With hindsight, some may claim it is now easy to say, but I still maintain that if Baldwin's fears had proven out, it would have been a short war indeed. On the whole, though, I don't believe Mussolini would have dared openly oppose Britain in a fight. Much of Britain's fleet, still then the largest in the world, was anchored at Alexandria. It could easily have blockaded Italy, preventing Italian troops and equipment from getting to Abyssinia, and there would have been insignificant loss, if at all, to Britain.

In any event, the strutting Italian dictator called Britain's bluff and won. What was even more important, Britain's ignominious crawfishing before the Duce obviously did not go unnoticed by Adolf Hitler. Long before Neville Chamberlain returned from Munich waving that infamous piece of paper before photographers, newsreel cameras and microphones, having signed away to Hitler the fate of Czechoslovakia and claiming to have secured "peace in our time," the peace at any price policy based on continued appeasement of the two leading Fascist dictators could still have been halted. And the impetus for that possibility came from a somewhat surprising quarter, Soviet Russia!

Mindful of the strong possibility that he would eventually have to fight Nazi Germany and the fact that his army was still limping back to recovery from the murderous purges he himself had instigated, Stalin had his man at the League of Nations, Maxim Litvinov, propose a three-power pact between the USSR, Britain and France to guarantee the sovereignty of Eastern European nations against further encroachment by an aggressive Germany. Had the Tri-Partite Proposition been acted upon, it may even have saved Czechoslavakia. But once more Britain dithered, France gandy danced, and the road to Hitlerian conquest of Eastern and Western Europe, Scandinavia, the Balkans, and, initially, much of North Africa lay wide open.

Thus was the scene set for World War Two. By the time it was over, more people had been murdered by Hitler's thugs in prisons and concentration camps throughout all the countries under the Nazi jackboot heel than there are people in Canada today. In the fighting, Russia lost more troops than there are Canadians in Canada today; Germany lost almost as many; and the flower of British and Commonwealth youth and much of that from the United States of America were decimated.

* * *

I cite all the foregoing in this chapter to serve as background for my own experiences and thoughts in much of the preceding chapters and because in 1989, shortly before I began this memoir, we marked the fiftieth anniversary of the outbreak of that war. Though much was written, said, and shown on television about that anniversary, including film footage from those times, I have neither seen nor heard, then nor since, much at all about the events I have just put forward. Yet I believe such things need to be said, not only in the context of the history of that time but also in the context of what I have set down in earlier chapters.

Furthermore, I began this memoir in the fall, which has long been my favourite time of year, as indeed it would seem it has become for my son. In the fall of 1939, I had not the remotest idea that, decades hence, I would be able to journey at this time of year into perhaps the most peaceful, certainly most awe-inspiring, part of the world I have ever ventured into and come to know—an area where one can fully recognize and appreciate what is meant by "God's groves, the trees; God's throne, the mountains."

Hunting for me is of secondary importance to the absolute joy of walking unhindered, often unaccompanied, through those groves; of being able to gaze, often for hours, at the majestic peaks and ramparts of that throne; of watching, often in lazy rather than alert fashion, the sweep of wild grass meadows, the flash of sun and moonlight on a mountain lake; of listening to the gurgle and the crash of untamed rivers; of seeing a myriad more stars than I can see in the same night sky over my home less than 400 miles away; of marvelling at the never still, ever undulating flashes of the Northern Lights; of hearing and, as I have also remarked upon hitherto, of literally being able to feel the Great Silence of the wilderness.

Half a century and more ago I never thought I would be so fortunate to be able to return to the land of my birth, let alone discover and come to live the greater portion of my life in this truly most magnificent of provinces.

As with most who fought and were directly involved in, or were in the path of, armies engaged in history's greatest and most terrible war, I never then really believed I'd be lucky enough to survive it. Conversely, undoubtedly because of the unbounded and often unfounded optimism of youth and young adulthood, I never really believed I would die in battle, much less out of battle in an air raid or by accident. I did sustain a couple of wounds, one fairly serious, but I survived none the worse.

I have seen death in many forms. Some gut-wrenching. Others unbelievably swift, where a comrade was alive one moment, an instant later gone to eternity. I have witnessed horribly, painfully slow death and, in some respects, even more terribly devastating woundings that mutilated and permanently crippled those suffering them.

Jax with Israeli unit prior to night patrol, Jax on left next to Colonel

During my time in German POW camps, I met and talked with German soldiers who wore that army's silver wounded medal, a decoration that denoted the man had suffered at least four wounds in battle and/or loss of one limb or an eye. Almost all of them who wore that decoration also wore the scarlet-and-silver-edged ribbon of the "Frostbite Medal"—meaning they had served at least one and more often at least two winter campaigns on the Russian front. The vast majority of those Germans were *Wehrmacht,* or regular Army, troops. I came into contact only rarely with SS troops and, with one exception, those contacts were not the most amenable. The exception was with SS Panzer General Sepp Dietrich in the Jimmy Donald incident.

I never had any regard for Nazi philosophy and politics any more than for Communist philosophy and politics, but by force of circumstances already related, I witnessed more of Hitlerianism before and during the war. It was a long time after the outbreak of that conflict before countries outside the Reich began to get an idea if not also, in German-occupied nations, direct experience of that philosophy and those policies in action. Furthermore, it was not until the end of the European war that the world came to realise the full scope of inhumanity and horror resulting from the same policies and twisted philosophy. To this day there are some who lived during those times who cannot comprehend, much less believe, such brutal bestialities could be visited upon millions upon millions of men, women and children by human beings of a nation that previously gave the world much in the arts, medicine, science and industry. This too in spite of the fact that one great German religious leader, Martin Luther, and one of the most popular composers, Richard Wagner, were both rabid anti-Jewish in many of their opinions and pronouncements.

It cannot be denied that some elements of the regular German Army and a number of its high-ranking career officers had a part in the brutish actions carried out against civilians in German-occupied areas. By and large, however, the Army played the deadly game of war generally according to the rules. Otherwise neither myself nor the great majority of military prisoners would have survived the war.

On the other hand, the SS played a major part in the terror and atrocities perpetrated against the so-called *untermenschen* or subhumans, which in the Nazi lexicon applied to creeds and races deemed inferior to the Aryan breed. That in itself was tragically ironic. The term Aryan, while supposedly denoting people of Nordic origin, stems from ancient East Indian lore. It is equally ironic, even farcically so, that the crooked cross, the swastika, adopted by Hitler and his gang is an ancient symbol from Hindustan.

A final irony arose from the Nazi claim that purity of their race was best illustrated by tall, well-developed, blond, blue eyed men and women. Yet the Nazi party was led by a covey of dark-haired, dark-eyed, mental and physical cripples: Hitler, Goebbels, Himmler, Rosenberg, Hess and Goering—the latter having the added distinction of being a sexual deviant. Nevertheless, the great majority of the German people of that era, if they didn't swallow the cretinous creed of these thugs in its entirety, did little or nothing until it was too late to challenge, much less stamp it out before it led to the destruction of their nation.

To perpetuate the Aryan myth, human stud farms were set up in various parts of pre-war Germany. There young SS men were coupled with fair German maidens to produce what the Hitler gang fervently believed would be the basis for their ranting Fuhrer's thousand-year Reich.

There were two main SS elements. The so-called *Waffen* or armed SS comprised fighting units, and the *Einsatzgruppen* set up and ran the torture chambers and death camps. Some postwar apologists, outside as well as inside Germany, for the Waffen SS have contended that as fighting units they had little or no part in mass murder, torturing and related atrocities. This is simply not true. In occupied countries and even in battle, Waffen SS troops carried out mass torture and outright murder against civilians and often against military prisoners, SS General Kurt Meyer's case involving the murder of Canadians captured in France after the invasion being only one such example.

It is also undeniable that Waffen SS units were formidable in battle, fanatically loyal to Hitler and Nazi philosophy. It is equally true those SS units invariably were supplied with the finest equipment and machinery with which to fight, often before or instead of Army groups and regiments. Yet, in many instances, the Army handled the toughest frontline fighting, while the SS got the accolades.

I had only the most cursory knowledge of such things when Sepp Dietrich visited the Stargard camp and was momentarily stymied by the sight of the naked and manacled Jimmy Donald. Later that day, our compound leader Tony Anthony and myself were ordered to report to the offices of the camp commandant. The offices were outside the camp proper, in a German barracks a mile or so from the camp itself. I forget now the reason for the order. As we were about to be returned, however, Dietrich, who had been in a meeting with camp officials, followed us from the commandant's office. He knew we had been taken at Dieppe and started talking to us and asking questions about Canada and Canadian life in general. Since I had not spent any time in this country beyond a few months after my birth, Tony carried that part of the conversational chore via my translating efforts. But when Dietrich moved into the area of politics and political philosophy, I got fully into the act. (I've long suffered verbal diarrhoea, which may account for any success I enjoyed before microphones and cameras in later life.)

The SS general and I engaged in what, at times, became a spirited discussion for about three quarters of an hour. Tony Anthony and a clutch of officers of the camp staff, army and SS who were part of Dietrich's retinue provided an interested if not also, at times, amused audience. Our exchange became sharp at one point in particular when I asked why Hitler had flatly refused to shake hands with the man who proved to be the world's fastest at the Berlin Olympics in 1936, the legendary Jesse Owens. As head of the host nation for those games, Hitler was required to meet and present medals to event winners. The handshake refusal made headlines around the world. In our conversation, Dietrich could not, or would not, give a direct answer but launched again into more Nazi philosophy, trying to press the claim that the Fuhrer had never intended to make war, particularly against Britain and her Commonwealth. All the standard rhetoric flowed forth about us Canadians being tools of the Jewish financial barons *etcetera* and so on *ad infinitum*.

Even so, it was an interesting exchange, all the more so when realizing the status of Tony and myself when ranged alongside that of the coterie of SS and army brass hats. One further incident intrigued me. As we two were dismissed, Dietrich returned our salutes with a military salute. Normally SS troops gave the extended-arm salute favoured by the Nazi party. At the time, about a year prior to the end of the war in Europe, neither Anthony nor myself had any idea of the depths of human degradation to which that twisted Party philosophy had already descended.

Dietrich was later to become Rommel's panzer commanding general in France immediately after the Normandy landing. His 1st SS Panzer Corps was involved in the initial invasion counters attacks and later in the battle for Caen—a battle in which Canadian troops distinguished themselves and, as we now know, in which occurred the incident referred to earlier when Meyer's troops, then under Dietrich's command, murdered those Canadian prisoners. Furthermore, as with almost all SS units then in France, undoubtedly men of the 1st Panzer Corps, if not Dietrich himself, rounded up and summarily executed hundreds of Army colleagues involved in, even only remotely suspected of involvement with, the plot to assassinate Hitler in July of the invasion year.

Continuing my retrospective, I have often wondered what happened to men of the calibre of Hauptmann Hauffe, commandant of our Canadian compound at Stargard. A punctilious officer in our dealings with him, he also had a decidedly wicked sense of humour (something of a rarity especially with the officer class of the German army). Shortly after Renwick, Hallaran *et al* and I were returned to Stargard following the Schonrade saga and some weeks prior to the incidents just related, I became Tony Anthony's official interpreter. That duty meant having direct and almost daily dealings with Hauffe.

One day I was ordered down to his office, which was inside the camp alongside the main gate. There I found two of our fellows who'd been nabbed by a guard when found wandering in the French compound. In my interpreter duty I had to explain to them why they had been arrested and was requested to ask them for an explanation. They had been trading with the French (strictly forbidden by camp rules), and they said that's just what they had been up to. It was then my role, to which I soon became, I thought anyway, efficiently accustomed, to indulge in outright lying. So I told Hauffe that the men had lost their way trying to return to our compound from the camp hospital. A weak alibi in retrospect, but it seemed to satisfy Hauffe, who passed along an expected warning about not letting it happen again. The men were returned with myself to our compound without them having to spend a few days in the cooler. I say again, not an isolated incident.

It was months later, as that year was drawing to a close, Hauffe surprised the you-know-what out of me one day by answering a series of questions of ours in excellent English. Took me a few minutes before I realised he was replying in English. I should not have been surprised, given that he had spent time more than two decades earlier in an English POW camp. I had been consistently lying to him through my early time as Canadian compound interpreter and he had known it all along, but until that particular day, I of course had no inkling he knew.

A short time later, not long before Christmas 1944, I myself was doing a 21-day stretch in the cooler as a result of a stupid mistake on my own part. I got into an argument with a belligerent guard near the main gate of the camp. He made some remark that touched me on the raw, and I replied by calling him an asshole, in German. He swung his rifle from his shoulder. I started to wrestle it from him. The guard NCO and another soldier dashed over, and into the cells I went. It was not exactly a novel experience. In fact, there were times when I welcomed the chance to be off in isolation. On that occasion, I was still inside at Christmas and was surprised when Hauffe appeared at my cell door Christmas Eve day.

I was ordered to accompany him to the Canadian compound, and that was all he said. Inside the compound he took me through every block. Each contained a large Christmas tree, all of 'em decorated with strips of the metallic substance dropped by our air forces on raids over Germany. I gather it had the ability to foil enemy radar. Our air force fellows called it "window" if I recall correctly. Lord knows where and how Hauffe came by the trees and that mount of "Christmas icicles!"

At the end of our tour, as we reached the compound gate, he said he felt I should be allowed to spend the Season with my comrades, but that I'd have those days added to the end of my sentence. He saluted, wished us all a Merry Christmas and, as he departed, said with a grin, "I told you, next year." When he was gone, it all came back to me. One day not long after the Normandy landings we had been discussing the progress of the war.

"And when do you think this war will be over?" he had asked me.

With great confidence, I replied, "Christmas of this year (1944)."

He shook his head. "No. Not this Christmas. But the next you will all be home with your families."

It wasn't long after that Christmas that we in Stargard could hear the sound of Russian guns as their armies continued their march westward. February of 1945 was but a few days old when we Canadians were told to pack what we could carry and then, one cold dawn, led by a German officer we'd never seen before, we began our own march westward. We learned that Hauffe had been shipped east, probably to be ground up in the inexorable drive of the Russian juggernaut. Enemies we may have been, but in the months I knew him, I came to know him as a gallant, gentlemanly German officer.

There were others. One fellow bore the somewhat unprepossessing name of Paul Klinkball. In his fifties then, he had been in the First War, an Uhlan cavalryman. He was in charge of our woods-working party the day I tasted, for the first and last time, rubbing alcohol, courtesy of our Russian friends. That old warrior delighted in coming into our compound of an evening, after his daily duties were over, to enjoy Canadian cigarettes and a cup or more of coffee, do a little trading and swap lies with us. Two infantry sergeants, both of whom came from the same mid-German village, had grown up together, joined the army at the same time, served in the invasion of the Low Countries, France and Russia, were both in the same regiment, both wounded a number of times, both minus an arm, one the left, the other the right arm. They said they'd left those limbs somewhere on the Russian steppes. One was dark haired, the other fair. Both were fellows of infinite jest. Both were in charge of guard detachments on a project involving a number of us in the town of Stargard the day Kimberley made good his escape.

On our return to camp that day neither of them said a word as we passed through the main gate, and they were promptly arrested. Both were court-martialed and we were later told shipped back to the then fast-shrinking Eastern Front from which, like millions of their comrades, they likely never returned. As we returned to the camp that day, while neither spoke as they were led away, they both nodded in our direction. I'm sure if they could have spoken they would have used a then familiar German phrase: *"So ist Das Krieg"* ("such is war").

* * *

"Jax" center,
reporting from Kennedy Platform Checkpoint Charlie 1967

More than two decades later, in the spring of 1967, I was to return to Germany for the first time since the war. I was on assignment, but I also took the opportunity, through the good offices of the Bonn government, to visit places I had seen pre-war. I was also able to visit the site of one of the camps to which I have referred in earlier chapters, Hohenfels.

The day I made that trip the German who accompanied me on behalf of the West German government was not someone I had met in my prior time at that camp. In fact, he was an infant when the war began. But, yet another irony of ironies, as we drove into the area, which was in the American occupation zone, he was held in the guardroom of the U.S. armoured unit billeted there, while I was escorted in the manner of a VIP to their headquarters to meet and talk with the senior U.S. officer. When I explained why I made the pilgrimage, he and his colleagues looked somewhat strangely at me. None said anything specific on the point, but I got the distinct impression they were thinking, *What sort of nut is this who wants to visit and tour around the site of an old POW camp?*

The U.S. unit was on manoeuvres that particular day but, typical of American hospitality, the commanding general halted the troop and equipment movements and for the next two hours drove me through the whole area. Almost nothing was left of the original camp structure and buildings except for concrete bases on which, back then, had stood the guard towers.

I stood alone for a while on the very spot where the cooler had been and from where MacDonald and I took off that May night twenty-four years earlier. A not unexpected nostalgia enveloped me for some time as I gazed south across the hills and valleys of the country we two had walked that first night. We never met again after the handful of us Canadians were shipped from Hohenfels to Stargard. Nor have we corresponded, even though at that time we promised so to do.

Before I left the Hohenfels area to continue my then legal journey south to Regensburg and ultimately on to Nuremberg and Munich, I was invited to raise a glass in the U.S. unit's regimental mess. Again the years fell away. The mess was in the building that previously housed the camp hospital. It was while there, suffering some minor ailment in the fall of '42, the manacle order caught up with me.

In the same hospital, incidentally, the senior British medical officer was Australian, a Major Brooke Moore. Aussies who knew him before we all came together at Hohenfels warned us he had a strange fixation. For some inexplicable reason, inexplicable to a majority of us anyway, he believed every man should have been circumcised as an infant. If not, he claimed it was still vitally necessary as a health measure. When and if a prisoner came under Brooke Moore's care he would go into his selling job. Not that many fell for it, including myself when I was in there.

Some weeks later, a New Zealander named Jim Welch, in civilian life a respected Kiwi newspaper cartoonist, I gather, who often sketched clever interpretations of various aspects of camp life, got word Brooke Moore was going out with a wood-working party in the nearby forest. The following morning, Welch's cartoon appeared on the main camp notice board. It depicted a grove of trees, a strip of bark cut from each one just above the place where they grew out of the ground. It needed no caption to illustrate to us that Brooke Moore had been out in the woods.

It's a curious thing, taking a journey back in time in one's mind, more so when a man makes a physical journey back as I did in 1967. The impact of returning to places I had been pre-war, when Nazism was in full bloom and cry, at times made me shudder inwardly. During the '67 trip I spent a few days at the Hotel Dreesen in Godesberg, a few miles from Bonn. Among other attributes, Godesberg is the birthplace of Beethoven. The Dreesen, a most comfortable hostelry, had more sinister recollections for me. The hotel, named after the family who ran it for many decades, backs onto the Rhine, providing a view across that historic river. On the other side, on top of a hill stands an old castle, still used on state occasions to lodge visiting dignitaries. Neville Chamberlain stayed there in late September of 1938. Hitler was staying at the Dreesen, the proprietor of which was a Nazi party luminary. Chamberlain met the German dictator in the Dreesen on that occasion; at that meeting the fate of Czechoslovakia was sealed, although the coup de grace was not administered until a few days later at the infamous Munich meeting.

The first evening I was at the hotel on my 1967 visit, I stood for some time looking out at the circular driveway, which was lined with sleek, generally black Mercedes limousines—a picture emblematic of West Germany's amazing postwar recovery. In my mind's eye, however, another scene was superimposed as I remembered the last time I had looked at that same driveway from across the street. It was lined on either side with black uniformed, black high-booted, black steel-helmeted SS troops. Their uniform sleeves carried silver-edged armbands on which was the Gothic scripted word *Leibstandarte*: Hitler's bodyguard.

It has been said that those who do not remember the past are fated to relive it, but my "black" mood that evening in 1967 gradually gave way to the realisation that only a few miles away stood the parliament of the postwar government of the Federal Republic of Germany, the first ever full-fledged experiment in parliamentary democracy the German nation has known. It is significant also to realize that, up to the present day, the experiment has lasted more years than any between-wars period in German history. It is to be sincerely hoped it will never die.

Some days later I was forcefully reminded that, even as there remains a thin geographical line between east and west Germany and eastern and western Europe, so also there remains the distinct line between democracy and suffocating totalitarianism. I was scheduled to do a broadcast from the Berlin wall direct to Vancouver. Until that time, it was the longest live transmission between that then still divided city and the Canadian west coast. Working with the West Berlin government, RIAS (Radio in the American Sector) of Berlin handled the technicalities for my hour-long broadcast from the Kennedy platform at the well-known Checkpoint Charlie. RIAS performed a superb technical job, enabling me not only to talk directly to my audience in this province but also to speak with listeners and answer their questions in an atmosphere that broadcast engineers delight in calling "studio quality." During the time I was on the air, West Berlin police and U.S. military authorities cleared the area of visitors and rubberneckers.

Not until I had finished the broadcast did I learn from the Americans and the police that also, throughout the full period of the broadcast, a shotgun microphone had been trained on me, and a film camera had been recording the performance from a building directly across from me, in the eastern sector—the side then under another suffocating totalitarian cloud, communism.

* * *

I am of course older now than I was even that relatively short time ago in 1967. Much older since the days I witnessed the suffocating Nazi cloud engulf Germany and most of Europe and seriously threaten democracy in the remainder of what was then the free world. With the passage of time, some things can be forgiven. Time, however, does not allow us to forget. I shall continue to recall and remember events and persons I have set before you with each subsequent passing year, counting myself so very fortunate to have known those years and events, counting myself even more fortunate to have survived events and years and still be able to reflect on it all in relative comfort and reasonable safety.

What better place for such reflections than sitting with my back to a tree in the Chilcotin highcountry? What better time of year so to do than "lovely fall" or, as John Greenleaf Whittier, an American poet of the last century, so aptly put it, the time of "the tints of Autumn, a mighty flower garden blossoming under the spell of the enchanter, frost"?

*El Arish oasis in Sinai where Israeli radar
set up to trap Libyan jet fighters*

LaVergne, TN USA
01 September 2009
156659LV00002B/162/A